A Simple Man Living in a Complex World

Life & Business:
Campfire Stories from the Asylum

Glen J. Carrio

Editor: Barbara Browning Carrio

Wild Dog Publishing
2455 Executive Circle
Colorado Springs, CO 80906
719.576.4571
FAX: 719.576.5640
email: info@carriocabling.com

Printed in the United States of America

ISBN: 978-0-9819365-1-2

This book is dedicated to my mom,

Jolene Smith, "Jo Jo,"

the greatest.

The best model of resourcefulness,

strength, and tenacity.

TABLE OF CONTENTS

TABLE OF CONTENTS

ACKNOWLEDGMENTS

I am deeply thankful to two individuals who made this book happen.

Thank you to Greg Snyder, the main man behind Incognito Marketing, who first encouraged me to write this book and prodded me again and again, and again and again, to get moving.

I am most grateful to Barbara Browning Carrio, an experienced and published writer, who became my written hand. By coincidence, timing, and God's grace, she also became my wife during the writing of this book. I may be able to speak relatively well, but writing is not a strength, along with reading and my favorite, spelling, all fallouts of living in a dyslexic world. Her understanding of me as an individual and as a businessman is a tremendous gift. Without her, this book would never have made it from the crowd of thoughts, images, and ideas in my mind to the pages of this book.

I'd also like to thank the following people (and others) for their inspiration:

Wally Jones
My mother, Jolene Smith
Robert Maxwell
Gene Roddenberry
Willy Wonka
Elvis Presley
Gene Day
Stuart Courtney
Porky Pig
Gigantor
Jonny Quest
The Man from U.N.C.L.E.
The Woman from U.N.C.L.E.
Illya Kuryakin
Emma Peel
John Steed
Roman Gabriel
"Speed Racer"
John Wayne
Clint Eastwood
Jesus
God Almighty
Holy Spirit
Luke
Milt Owens

Oz
Boris Spassky
Ronald Reagan
Kato (Bruce Lee), *The Green Hornet*
Dennis Conner
Tom Whidden
Ron Dennis
Ayrton Senna
Frank Williams
Jim Hall
Jackie Stewart
J. Vernon McGee
Fawn Hall
Oliver North
Judge Robert Bork
Gary Gabelich
Don Garlits
Tim Williamson
Mel Fisher
Ron Howard
My sixth-grade teacher, Mr. Doezema
Mike Colver
George Cardas
Gary & Linda Emmick
Harry "Fruitloops" Wilms

I was born Glen Joseph Williams in Glendale, California. The way I heard the story, I should have been a Carrio from conception, but my Spanish ancestors feared discrimination and wanted to blend into American society when they arrived in the U.S. Of course, that's the story from my dad, who had a habit of telling stories that many times, shall we say, were embellished. My mom explains that my great-grandmother, Marie Carrio, simply married a Williams.

Either way, when I was about 21 years old, I decided to take my great-grandparents' Spanish surname and changed my name to Glen Joseph Carrio.

A big focus of my life as a young boy and into my late teens was go-kart racing. It was a bigger priority than just about anything else, girls included. I was always driven to succeed, loved competition, and was into the mechanical and strategic aspects of racing. For a couple of years, I raced go-karts with my mom and my sister. How many guys can say that?

After surviving the high school years, I went straight to work. In my late 20s, I decided to start a company and build cables, connectors, and other crazy things. Carrio Cabling Corporation (www.carriocabling.com) celebrated its 25th anniversary in 2013. We were "lean," "world class," "just in time," "TQM," "Statistical Process Control (SPC)," and "Six Sigma" before these were buzzwords, even when it was just me and a couple of machines in a 1,000-square-foot space in Signal Hill, California. Our philosophy is simple: If You Touch it, Finish It.™

In life and in business, many things have happened that have challenged a simple man like me. The challenges are doubly so in today's business environment where "How cheap can we make it?" has nearly everyone rushing to China like lemmings to the sea, or perhaps it's more like rats to a feeder bar. But I'm still here. I figured I could either give up or stay on track.

I like to think I'm the same guy I was at age 11 when I ran my first go-kart race on a track in southern California and the same guy I was at age 28 when I started this company—just a guy building things, making them the best every time, and not cutting corners or selling my soul to the outsource, off-shore demon. In many ways, I feel as though I'm just a kid trying to win a go-kart race and trying to win it the right way.

Why did I write a book of stories, what I like to think of as campfire tales? For several reasons: (A) Much of the core of what Carrio Cabling is today is based on personal experiences, opportunities, and things I learned years ago. (B) We don't need another boring business book. (C) Some of the very best companies in the world, American businesses, continue to miss the boat on efficiency and therefore needlessly put themselves at a competitive disadvantage in the U.S. and global marketplaces. And (D) people often ask, "How'd you get started doing this, anyway?"

Perhaps these stories will answer that question, capture a few of the fundamental principles I've tried to live by and build this business around since Day 1, and be a spark for U.S. inventors and designers to look for new ways to break the cycle of creating new ideas, only to have some overseas company reap the manufacturing financial rewards.

For Carrio Cabling's current, future, and prospective customers, and for other American manufacturers, I hope this book inspires you to stay on point, stay true to your core principles, and keep doing what you do best. We have a way to go in educating customers and American consumers about the true cost of "China price." However, regardless of what happens in the global marketplace, perceptions of value, and pricing, there is nothing, anywhere, like Yankee ingenuity.

Chapter 1:
Karting, Exploring, Building

Chapter 1:
Karting, Exploring, Building

First Go-Kart Race: Under the Lights at Adams

BE PREPARED TO WIN.

Being prepared to win—really prepared, not just kind of, mostly, or nearly prepared, but 100% prepared—is one of *the* most basic keys to being competitive in business, or in any field for that matter. I learned this lesson many Earth rotations ago, as an 11-year-old kid who was crazy about go-karting; and, like so many of us, I learned it the hard way. Years later, when my son was racing go-karts and then formula cars, one of the reasons we were successful was that I had failed.

In racing, there are at least three things that are imperative if you want to have any shot at winning:

- Have more information than anyone else—about the track, your competitors, every detail imaginable about your own equipment, and your support team, if you're lucky enough to have one.
- Look ahead to what could go wrong—because something always goes wrong—and leave nothing to chance.
- Be the first one at the track.

The first go-kart race I ever competed in was at night. The lighting wasn't that good. I was 11 years old, I had my go-kart, and I wanted to race.

I always wanted to race. I spent many hours driving around a dirt field on the ranch where I lived with my family. Then one day, I saw a go-kart track from the freeway. It was Adams Race Track, in Riverside, California, which became a famous track for go-karting years later. My parents would drop me off, and I'd spend the whole day there practicing and testing.

Then one day I said, "I want to race," so my mom took me to this night race at Adams.

Our family was poor, so my go-kart was old. My dad called it "Tobacco Road" because it was so ratty. I think my dad found it through an ad in the newspaper. I loved it when I first saw it—square tubing, not round, and a smell that to this day still inspires me: the smell of castor oil.

When I arrived at the race, I looked around and was intimated right out of the chutes. The first thing that crossed my mind was, "I'm not prepared." Number one, at a very basic level I was late. There were a dozen kids in line in front of me at the registration check-in, and I could hear the Rrrrr-aaaa---rrrrr of engines, which told me my competitors were already on track, testing. Second, my go-kart was not up to scratch in any way. It was clean, because I always kept it clean, but I could see right away that it was not that good and I was not ready the way the other guys were. They had all kinds of tools and spares and were highly organized. I had a miniature tool box, an old gas can, and a tire pump. That was it.

That was my first lesson, that night at age 11 in southern California, about the cost of not being prepared. It wasn't that I didn't have the super-painted helmet or that I was afraid. No. I was upset because, quite simply, it was clear, "I'm not prepared for this."

I had nothing but mechanical problems that night. The source of the problem was one little screw. A 4/40 screw came out, and it messed up the throttle and the throttle wouldn't work.

4/40 Pan Head Screw
Actual Size

I not only failed to finish in the top half, I finished last or second to last. The first thoughts that ran through my mind at the end of the race were, "How can I make sure that never happens again? And why is it that I didn't check every single nut, screw, and bolt on that stupid go-kart?" It would have taken very little time to check everything. I could have done it in 10 minutes or less: Take out my wrenches and my screwdriver. Then clean, check, tighten; clean, check, tighten. That was *the* most basic thing. I got my ass kicked that night because I didn't take care of one little thing: one 4/40 screw.

After the race, I was packing up and crying. My mom was there. She felt bad because she thought I was upset about losing, but that wasn't it. I *was* upset with myself for not being prepared. In that moment, I swore never again would I not be prepared. I would never be in that situation again.

About three weeks later, in the second go-kart race of my life, I was prepared and I annihilated everyone, winning my first race.

It was great to win. It's always great to win. But it wasn't about winning then, and it's not about winning today. People say, "What do you mean, 'It's not about winning?' Isn't that the point? You have to think positively."

To say, "I will never lose another race" is obviously ridiculous, just like it's ridiculous to say, "Carrio Cabling will never lose another bid." The point is that you have to be smart enough to know that you can't *win* every race, but you can be *prepared* to win every race. You *must* do your homework. You *must* study.

I'm also not saying, "We're all winners, and you are a winner even though you finished last," like those silly ribbons schools and other organizations give a kid for just being a "participant" in a competition.

My favorite race was a race I didn't win. I remember it perfectly in my mind. What made it my favorite race was that I did everything right: I was completely prepared, I went for the win, and I led on and off for a while, so I was competitive. In other words, it was a great race. But I finished second.

Someone might say, "That's not the right attitude for a kid to have in a competition!" Actually, it is. I wanted to kick those guys' butts and I *tried* to win. I came up a little short, but I was not upset about it because I was flat-out prepared. I did it all. I would hope that every kid would go into every competition prepared, doing his or her best, and trying to win, trying to prevail, but proud of whatever score he or she gets, whatever the final outcome.

In terms of being prepared, I really should have known better, even before that first race. I always thought I was a kid who was prepared, and I wasn't even a Boy Scout. I just was prepared, but I didn't become someone who was committed to being 100% prepared—in other words, I didn't get it in my bones—until I lost that race.

Racehorse Ranch Exploring

THINK AHEAD.
STAY CURIOUS.

Before I started racing go-karts and just when I began to race, I lived on a racehorse ranch in southern California with my mom, my crazy dad, my sister, and my brother. The ranch was a great place for exploring, building, and thinking.

The reason we lived on this ranch was that my dad had gotten a job managing it. Not that he had any experience managing a ranch, let alone a racehorse ranch, but that's how it was with my dad. He believed his own lies so thoroughly that he could convince any potential employer that he could do anything.

One of my favorite days on the ranch was Saturday, but not for the reason most kids look forward to Saturday. I didn't want to sleep in or lie around watching television. I wanted to get up early, get outside, and go exploring.

School was hard for me. The teachers thought I was stupid and couldn't learn because I couldn't read. They were right that I couldn't read, but I like to think they might have been wrong about the stupid part.

Years later, I discovered that I'm dyslexic. Just about everything about school was difficult for me, especially reading, writing, and spelling. Since education is based so much on these skills and not so much on other ways of learning, my K–12 years were pretty much a disaster. When I was growing up, the prevailing wisdom was that intelligence was measured by how well one could read, write, and spell. Since I struggled greatly with all three of these "basics," my teachers, the principals, and just about every single educator I came into contact with thought I was stupid or "slow" or that I simply had a bad attitude.

Spelling tests were particularly challenging. On Monday, the teacher would list the words for the week on the board, which would be tested on Friday. It didn't take long to realize that the words on the test were in the exact same order as the words he had written on the board on Monday. That was my saving grace. "Regular" people, I'm told, see individual words in their minds. For me, it's an entirely different thing. The only way I passed a spelling test in school was that I memorized the list as a picture, with the letters in a specific order, row after row. Of course, when the teacher mixed it up and put the words in a different order or used words from previous tests, I was SOL. These basics are still challenging for me today, although I've come a long way from those school days.

6th Grade
Spelling Test
The Final

	Correct Spelling
Abalisleh	abolish
Ailmente	ailment
camofaluge	camouflage
depree	debris
Laquerae	lacquer
Silowet	silhouette
weaveal	weevil
holesale	wholesale
WomaN	women
"O"	zero

½/10

½-point credit for "woman" vs. "women"

F

Because school wasn't exactly a joy ride, I looked forward to Saturdays. The ranch was a great place for exploring—some 32 acres nestled in Jurupa Valley, California, with lots of fields, barns, all manner of equipment, cattle, chickens, dogs, geese, ducks, and, of course, racehorses, as well as the largest pile of manure I've ever seen in my life; it was a near hill it was so huge.

The ranch was in an area that was semi-rural, which seems odd for Southern California from today's point of view, but those were the days when there were miles and miles of open space. Living there was at once scary, wild, and exciting. Scary and wild because there was so much unknown. Exciting for the same reason. There was a certain wonder to the place. The number of things to investigate seemed nearly limitless.

The night before I'd go exploring, I'd think about the basic plan: where I might want to go, areas unknown, uncharted lands. I'd also think about what to take.

At the top of the list was my pellet gun. Obviously, if you're a kid, you *have* to take your pellet gun if you go out into untamed lands because, of course, you never know what might happen. For one thing, there were the alleged wild dogs. I never saw any, but I was told they were always there, running around somewhere, so I carried my pellet gun in the event I ran into one of them or some other unforeseen event.

Wild Dog Ready to Bite

Mine was a Czechoslovakian pellet gun that I had found at a pawn shop. The guy said it was from Czechoslovakia, and I thought, "How exotic is that?" Since it was natural for me to keep things prepped and cleaned, of course my pellet gun had to be prepped and cleaned every Friday night.

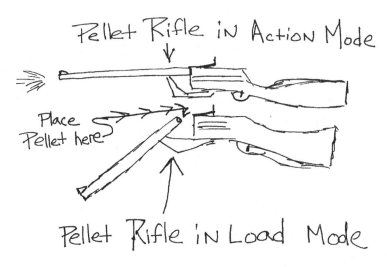

I also thought about how long it would take to get wherever I'd decided to go. The places I wanted to check out were usually a ways off and since I walked to wherever it was, it could take a couple of hours or more to get there. I figured if it was going to take me that long, I'd need snacks, so I prepared snacks and got out my canteen with the odd military smell and filled it with water.

I also had a utility belt, because, like my pellet gun, I figured every kid had to have a utility belt. I put all kinds of things in that belt. Pellets and BBs of all sorts were at the top of the list. Every kid, every boy at least, wants to fire darts or shoot pellets or BBs at abandoned buildings, hills, telephone poles, old cans, fence posts, the ground, the air, you name it. I always made sure to take two types of pellets, concave and convex, along with some BBs in the event of an emergency, meaning I had run out of pellets. BBs were the second choice for shooting anything because they were too small for my pellet gun. If I had to use BBs, I could only shoot straight ahead or diagonally upward. If I aimed downward in any way, the BBs simply rolled out.

I also put matches in my utility belt, a ski mask to conceal my identity in the event I ran into any nasty guys, and spares of this and that in case of a failure of some kind. I thought, "What if I get cold? What if it rains? What if...? What if...? What if...?" I also took a miniature can of breath spray. In combination with a lit match, it was instantly the world's smallest flame thrower, which could come in handy. I would have taken Aqua Net hair spray for the same purpose, but the can was too large to fit in my utility belt.

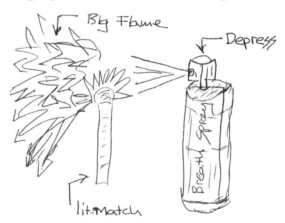

After I had everything together, I'd lay it all out in my bedroom: my pellet gun, my canteen, snacks, my utility belt, and whatever clothes I was going to wear. I'd go to bed at 9:30 or 10:00. My goal was up by 5:00, out by 5:15 before the parents got up. Long before the days when visualization became popular, I'd lie in bed and concentrate really hard on the number 5, and think, "I'm going to wake up at 5:00 a.m." Since everything was laid out, all I had to do in the morning was put my clothes on, climb out the upstairs window, crawl across the roof, jump onto the top of the cinder block wall, run along the edge, jump to the ground, and go exploring.

I would just go off walking. At the time, the land was largely undeveloped so there were many farms around and lots of fun things to do. I followed railroad tracks; explored barns, old buildings, and water tanks; and learned to smell a dead animal from a good distance. For the most part, I explored by myself and rarely ran into anyone. Later when I had a mini-bike, I increased my range. I was always curious, What's out there?

My natural curiosity was honed on the ranch and my thrill at discovering some new "find"—charred vegetation from brush fires, a cutting blade that hooked to the side of the tractor, a tank where the horses could swim, equipment of all kinds—never dampened. This time in my life set a precedent for exploration and discovery, which opens the eyes, whether in life or in business, to see seemingly unrelated events and issues differently.

Gadgets, Inventions, and Stuff

INVESTIGATE, APPLY, INVENT, BUILD.

My at-least-weekly ranch treks were a high priority. The other thing that was at the top of the list of great things to do was analyzing, probing, disassembling, and assembling just about anything.

I took many things apart as a kid. I think it's a common thing for boys to take gadgets and other mechanical things apart and put them back together again or at least try to put them back together. The first thing I remember taking apart was a pink electric can opener when I was about 8 years old. My mom walked in and said, "What have you done?!" I put it back together and it worked.

Like other boys, I loved helmets, particularly one I found in an old, black leather trunk that belonged to my dad. The trunk was usually locked, but one day it was open, so I looked inside and pulled out this helmet. It was green inside and had a soft lining like calfskin. It smelled old ... a bit of dust, leather, and wiring. My dad told me he wore it as a fighter pilot in World War II flying the "Red Ass" into battle. The other explanation was that he wore it when he flew transport planes in Alaska when my parents were first married but before I was born. This explanation made more sense because the helmet was nothing like the leather helmets I'd seen John Wayne and Gregory Peck, respectively, wear in the war movies *Twelve O'Clock High* and *Flying Tigers*, which were made about the early WWII era. It looked more like the hard helmet Jimmy Stewart wore in *Strategic Air Command*, set in the early 1950s.

The helmet may very well have been from my dad's time in Alaska, but I learned from my mom that he didn't fly planes in Alaska, nor did he fly any plane into battle during World War II, let alone one called the "Red Ass." He apparently did work as an air traffic controller in Alaska, however, so perhaps that's where he "found" the helmet.

Regardless of the true origins of the helmet, it intrigued me to no end. It had many parts that I studied endlessly. I loved wearing it. There was no question that when I put it on, I could run faster. I wore it all over the place for a couple of years, even to school. I eventually traded it to a neighbor kid for a G.I. Joe, which made my dad irate.

I was always curious how things were made and loved trying to discern their purpose. One of the big mysteries was a box I found one day when I was out walking. It was yellow and said "Bower plate." Inside the box was a cast aluminum part about the same size as the box. It had several threaded holes in it, as though it was supposed to be attached to something else. The box with the Bower plate sat on my desk in my room, and I kept trying to figure out where it went. Hopefully some day I would know, but meanwhile I could not comprehend how this thing was used. It bothered me that I couldn't figure it out, because I thought I should have known everything about every piece of equipment and every part ever made. I figured when I died and hopefully went to heaven, I would ask God, "What *was* that thing I found?"

Disassembling and assembling all kinds of appliances and garage finds was closely related to my other favorite pastime on the ranch: building and inventing. I was always making things: swords, different types of bikes, and devices of all kinds. One of my favorite things that I built, my wind-propelled wagon, was sparked in part by my frustration with the strong winds that would kick up in the afternoon on the ranch.

The dry wind also was the source of my first run-in with static cling, which bothered me to no end and still does to this day. Static cling is at the top of my list of "Top 10 Most Hated Things," along with droopy socks and imitation butter. (Plastic, butter-flavored popcorn topping, anyone?)

Static cling has always been at the top of my "most hated" list for a number of reasons. For one thing, my hair and clothes were always sticking to everything. My mom would drive me to school in the morning; as I walked from the house to the car I'd wear a helmet—but a different helmet from the one I found in my dad's trunk—to keep my hair from flying every which way and sticking to my face. I also hated touching anything infected by static electricity because of the sparks.

These early run-ins with static cling, something that was nothing but an unbelievable aggravation at the time, paid dividends in business years later. In go-karting we used fuel additives, in particular propylene oxide, nitromethane, and toluene, all of which have low flash points and can ignite in the blink of an eye. Similarly, static electricity can easily damage electrical products, so anti-static and static control processes and materials are a top priority in manufacturing.

The wind and all of its challenges frustrated me for these reasons, but it occurred to me that I ought to turn these frustrations into some kind of advantage. What's that old expression? If you can't beat 'em, join 'em. One day I had the idea to turn my regular, old wagon into a very cool wind-propelled wagon. So I built a sail from some old bed sheets, mounted it on the proverbial red wagon, and used the wind to propel me.

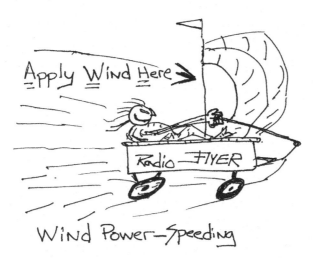

Apply Wind Here →

Radio FLYER

Wind Power—Speeding

There was a large aluminum gate, some 20 feet wide, which spanned the entrance to the ranch. I'd seen it pulse in the wind and figured, "If it pulses in the wind, it should cushion my hit." I thought I would bail out if the wagon went too fast, but either way, I could crash it into the gate as a brake.

I sat in my red wagon, checked the wind direction, directed the sail, and the wagon took off. I liked the speed of it and figured, "No problem. As I'm coming up to the gate, it will do exactly what I think it will do." I hit the gate at 5–6 mph, not that fast, but it was fast enough to prove my point that the wind could push me in my wagon.

Even though I eventually had a mini-bike, I always kept that wagon perfectly clean and tuned. Not much later in life, the very same wagon became a war wagon. My dad made sure everyone thought our family had incredible wealth. The truth was that we just got by. Because we didn't have much money, I tended to keep my toys a long time or morph them into other things.

After we lived on the ranch a few years, we moved to a suburban area near the University of Redlands in Redlands, California. I had seen the John Wayne film *War Wagon*, so it dawned on me that I had a wagon and therefore, of course, I should turn it into a war wagon. Sure enough, I built a war wagon.

I was always looking for some magical tool, part, or piece of whatever in the garage or somewhere in the barn, something that could be used for something else that was really cool. There was always something out there. The same was true for the war wagon.

There were some wooden crates laying around from the nearby citrus groves. One day, I looked at my red wagon and realized that two crates would fit perfectly inside the width of the wagon, so I put those in the bottom of the wagon. Then I made a lookout on the top of my wagon out of a metal canister I had found. There was also this weird material I stumbled on one day in an alley; it looked like simulated tile. I thought it was interesting and that I could probably jump on it and not break it, so I put that all over the outside of my wagon.

Sure enough, it all worked really well. I could throw rocks at my war wagon. I could shoot it with my pellet gun. I could get it wet. I could pop my head out of the metal part on top and look around. And I could get down inside and hide out, so when I got into trouble and my brother wanted to try to beat me up, which was just about all the time, I'd jump into my war wagon. He'd kick it over and jump on it and curse and spit at me, but he couldn't hurt me because I was inside.

WAR WAGON

Fast forward 6 to 8 years: The war wagon was still around, so I spray-painted it black and converted it into a "starter wagon," which my friends and I used to start go-karts.

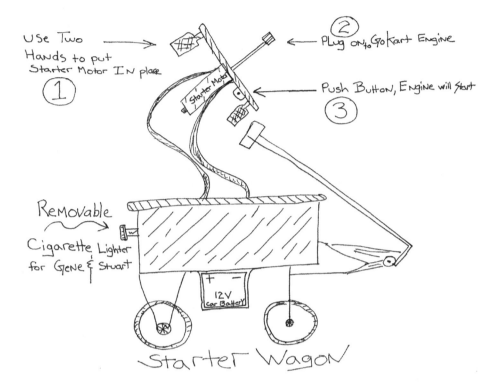

Chapter 2:
Carlson Hardware and Wally's Basement

Chapter 2:
Carlson Hardware and Wally's Basement

In ninth grade, I was in school, but racing go-karts at every opportunity. When I was younger, my dad felt guilty—about me, about my mom, about life, who knows—so he paid for my racing. By the time I was about 14, he lost his sense of guilt and didn't want to pay for racing anymore, so I started working at Carlson Hardware in Redlands, California, to make money for racing. My mom worked there, too.

Every day after school and on Saturdays, I went to work at Carlson's. When summer arrived, I worked 39 hours a week, because the owner said that if I worked 40 hours a week, he'd have to pay me minimum wage. The truth was that I was paid for 39 hours a week, but worked many hours more than that each week. I worked just below minimum wage for the next three to four years, all the way through high school and for a few months after graduation.

At the time I didn't see my job at Carlson's as anything more than a way to make money. In retrospect, working there provided a great deal more than that.

Icemaker Hook-ups and Toilet Leak Fun

LISTEN. ASK QUESTIONS.
FIND OUT IN ADVANCE WHAT THE CUSTOMER
REALLY WANTS.
GIVE THE CUSTOMER MORE VALUE, FREE OF CHARGE.

It was the time in America's history when icemakers were starting to be installed in refrigerators, so people always came into Carlson's who needed to hook up their icemaker. Some of my best work was with icemakers.

It was usually the wife who had sent her husband. "Honey, go get the stuff to hook up the icemaker." The guy would walk in and say, "I need to hook up my icemaker." That's usually all I had to go on. And if he had nothing more to say than that, I knew I was in trouble because I could not satisfy him.

He would say, "It isn't that complicated. There's obviously some plumbing somewhere on one end, and there's plumbing on the other end that you're going to connect with. Everybody knows . . . it's 1/4-inch copper tubing."

"Not necessarily."

"Well, everybody knows . . . all you need is a saddle valve."

"Ok, well, do you have any kind of pipe sticking out of the wall?"

"Yeah."

"Ok, is it a galvanized pipe? Is it a copper pipe? Or is it copper tubing?"

I'd start this line of questioning.

If he brought in any pieces, or called in advance, I could ask other questions. "Can you draw a picture of it? How close is the refrigerator to the water supply?" and so on.

At some point, we'd get into gender—which parts were male and which were female. It was always interesting when he finally got it. The guy would look down, light up, and say, "Ohh . . . I see. I understand how that works now. That's right."

Eventually I'd realize I was going to have to take a different tack in terms of the icemaker hook-up. I'd ask, "How far away do you live?"

Usually it wasn't too far, so I'd say, "Here's what I'm going to do. I'm going to sell you some copper tubing, which will be perfect for your situation. And I'm going to sell you the connections you need. However, since you're not sure what your specific connections are, I'm going to let you take some other parts with you.... I'm not going to charge you for them....and then see which ones look like this. Then bring back what you don't need. I'm really sorry. You're going to have to come back."

In essence, I front-end loaded by giving the customer a series of parts that might work when he got home.

Invariably, the guy would come back in and say, "I'll be damned! You were right. You know, on *this* side, it looks like this one, but over here....it looks like that. I never knew that." Then I'd take back the parts he didn't need. I'd never see him again, at least not about his icemaker.

It goes to the genesis of what we do at Carrio Cabling today: Give the customer what he really needs, not what he thinks he needs, and give him physical things.

The next time the guy came into the store, it was likely to be about the toilet. Usually the problem was the filler tube that runs from the water valve to the tank.

He would say, "You'll never guess what happened with my toilet this weekend."

"The little filler pipe came out at one end of the tank and flooded your bathroom."

"How did you know that?"

"Oh. .....I just guessed. You had a surge."

I'd start to ask him about his specific toilet, but eventually he'd ask, "Does it matter?"

"Well, does the valve look like this one? ...Or does it look this one?...Or more like this one?"

"No, it doesn't look like any of them."

"Does it look like this one?"

"Yeah, that's more like it."

"Ok......this stuff is really old, isn't it?"

"Yeah, how did you know?"

"Because it's so old, what's going to happen.....I'm really sorry to tell you this...When you tighten it down, it's going to crack, so I recommend that you take this, this, and this because it's going to break."

"No, that's okay. I don't need those things."

"Well, I just want to make sure you have what you need. It's about 50 cents, a dollar more, but I want to make sure you have what you need."

"No. I don't need it." He wanted to spend as little money as possible. Unfortunately, it was rather short sighted because now the guy's entire Saturday afternoon was going to be wasted driving back and forth to Carlson Hardware.

Every time, the guy would come in and say, "Damn! You were right. Man, the thing is leaking even *more*. I should have paid the buck for that stupid thing you were talking about."

I wouldn't want to make him feel any worse, so I'd say, "Well, no problem. At least now you'll get it fixed and you won't have to come back on your Saturday again and you're done."

Sometimes when the guy wouldn't want to spend the extra 50 cents or a dollar, I would try to avert the problem I knew was coming by saying, "I'll modify your filler tube pipe right now using this special pipe we sell. I'll modify it here in the store and you won't have to buy a tool you'll use only once. I'll just do it for you because I'd like to see you get it fixed once and for all."

I have customers today who get irritated when I ask lots of questions. "What's it going to be used for? Will it get wet? Will it vibrate?" etc. So often the response is, "You don't need to know that."

"Well, actually I *do* if you want me to give you what you need."

For example, one of our customers is a company we have been working with for about three years. Not long ago, we called our contact at the company and said, "You've asked us for some things that are probably not good for you, so we'd like to talk with you about that."

The answer was, "No. That's product number 51-73-6-4.1.1.000005/A. It's just a connector. Don't waste my time."

Fine. The meeting was over in 6–7 minutes. I can't do great work for a company like that; I can't help them.

I like to think of all of our interactions with customers as a conversation. Asking questions upfront shortens the conversation and leads to a much better result in terms of product delivery, customer satisfaction, profitability on both sides, and the customer getting exactly what he or she needs.

Opportunity Shows Up in a Military Olive-drab Jumpsuit

YOU NEVER KNOW WHERE
WHAT SEEMS LIKE A CRUMMY JOB MIGHT LEAD.

Working at Carlson Hardware was the time that I met all kinds of interesting people—people who changed my life. You might say that sometimes opportunity shows up in the craziest ways. For me, it was a guy in a military jumpsuit wearing a truss.

One day this guy came walking into the hardware store wearing a beret and three pairs of glasses. The first set of glasses was on straight. He had the other two pairs on top of the first pair, so the three pairs somehow served as multiple focal points. He was wearing a military jumpsuit, which at the time I thought was avocado green, perhaps because living in California there were avocado trees—and avocado-green kitchens—everywhere. Later I learned that the right term is "olive drab." Along with the olive-drab jumpsuit, he was wearing military boots, but he hadn't laced the boots all the way up. He only had a single lace at the top and one at the extreme bottom, so the tongues flopped when he walked.

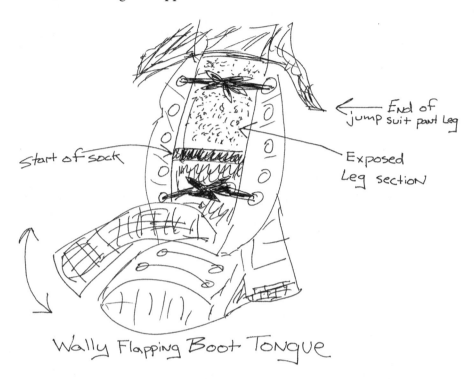

Wally Flapping Boot Tongue

The most compelling part of his outfit was the external truss he was wearing, which he had painted avocado green because, I later learned, avocado green was his favorite color. He'd taken a round piece of metal, a disk-shaped object about 2–3 inches in diameter, and painted it avocado green. Then he'd made a stainless steel clip that hooked around his leg. The disk-shaped metal piece, which looked like a large dot, was in just the right location, which happened to be very close to, shall we say, key male anatomy. I eventually learned that his name was Wally Jones. I waited on Wally several times while I worked at Carlson's during high school.

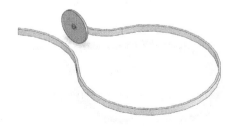

After graduation, I worked at Carlson Hardware for a few more months, but I needed to make more money. Gene Burgess, one of the great guys I worked with at Carlson's, knew someone working at a convalescent hospital, so I got a job there working as a janitor during the day at a much better rate of pay. At night, I took a three-month machine shop course at the local junior college. I mopped during the day, machined at night.

One day, I was at the convalescent hospital having a lunch break, and all of a sudden the door swung open where I was sitting and Wally walked in. He was still wearing the jumpsuit, the beret, the truss, the boots—the complete ensemble—minus the three pairs of glasses. He said, "Are you Glen?" I said, "Yeah." He said, "I've been looking for you."

Now mind you, I hadn't seen him in a couple of years. It had been some time. Again he said, "I've been looking all over for you." Then he handed me an inch-thick stack of paper with a phone number written on the top. He said, "Just call me," turned, and walked away.

In the stack of paper were all the patents that he had for everything from radar jamming used in World War II to the spotlights used for anti-aircraft to electrical and semiconductor inventions. I looked over these papers at lunch, thinking, "I have no clue what this is about," but I was intrigued. I called him and said, "Hey, this is kind of interesting." He said, "Why don't you come on over to my house?"

To The Basement

ANYONE CAN GAIN KNOWLEDGE.
THE MAGIC IS IN APPLYING IT.

A few days later, I drove to Wally's house in Redlands. He was working and living in the basement of a Victorian house in the middle of an orange grove. The house was owned by his girlfriend, Virginia, who lived in Long Beach, but owned this house as well. Virginia had a habit of buying things from yard sales; sometimes she would buy the entire yard sale, sight unseen. The upstairs of this house was used to store boxes of Virginia's purchases.

Apparently Wally was an inventor for Westinghouse years earlier, and he had all kinds of ideas he was working on in the basement. He wanted me to work with him to come up with more ideas and build equipment. He had multiple machines sitting around that he had built out of everything from car parts to scrap metal, and everything was painted, of course, avocado green. In fact, he had a specific Krylon number that everything had to be painted.

For instance, he showed me the avocado green hairpin machine, which, he said, was his crowning achievement. The machine made all kinds of weird noises as it continuously fed wire from a large spool about three feet in diameter, weighing 300-plus pounds, then cut and bent the wire into U-shaped hardware parts for a company manufacturing concrete prefabricated homes. The parts slipped into wet concrete to help hold the insulation in place on the walls.

Hair PiN

It wasn't long before I left my janitorial job at the convalescent hospital and started working in Wally's basement.

All of the guys I knew back then seemed to have some crazy vehicle. Wally had two crazy vehicles. One was a white Econoline van that was trashed out. It was the "go-find-pieces-of-junk" mobile for hauling metal and parts and other things to make machines. He also had the Stickymobile.

There was a guy in San Diego back then named Captain Sticky. His real name was Richard Pesta, but he called himself Captain Sticky. I'd seen

Sticky on TV the year before in a show called *Real People*. Sticky had taken a Lincoln Continental Mark V, painted it red, white, and blue, and put stars and stripes on the side along with "Captain Sticky, Destroyer of Evil." Then he put a smoke-colored plastic bubble on top and drove around southern California with a cape, campaigning for consumer causes and trying to stop injustices.

I found this great comic created by Jay Allen Sanford, a talented San Diego-based cartoonist and writer, about Captain Sticky and all of his good deeds.

©Jay Allen Sanford 2007. Reprinted by permission of Jay Allen Sanford.

Wally somehow had come into possession of the Stickymobile. The Stickymobile came complete with what Wally called the "golden gloves." I thought, "What do you mean?" So I looked in the back seat and there were workers' gloves—spray-painted gold—hanging from Sticky's utility belt. The white Econoline van and the Stickymobile were the two primary vehicles for what Wally called Wally Jones Industries.

Between projects, Wally wanted me to tunnel underneath the house. Virginia had just purchased what must have been 500 or more teak deck chairs from the *Queen Mary*, a British cruise liner in service from 1936 until 1969, when the city of Long Beach, California, purchased it and later turned it into a hotel. Wally wanted me to make space for Virginia to store the chairs and other yard-sale treasures.

He also said that Virginia would come down from time to time and that she would want to have group sessions. He made it clear that part of my job description was to go upstairs and sit with Virginia and talk about her problems and everybody else's in the neighborhood. I told him it was unproductive, and I stayed out of it.

In addition to hiring me, Wally decided to employ an old mechanic friend of his, Robert Maxwell, whom we both called "Maxwell." Maxwell flew P-38 fighters from one island to another in the Pacific during WWII, but he never saw combat. Wally had met him in a junkyard in Los Angeles. Whereas Wally had his avocado green truss, Maxwell wore a belt that was a rope, like Jethro Bodine wore in *The Beverly Hillbillies*. His vehicle was a 1952 Rambler Americana station wagon. He had put a round gun turret on the top to take panoramic pictures, which he then tried to sell to whoever would buy them.

Maxwell worked with me in Wally's basement. He was a jack of all trades. He did everything. He was full of energy and had a great voice, which Wally always said sounded like a fog horn.

Wally and Maxwell would say, "Glen, you've got to go into town to get supplies," which might include going to Carlson Hardware, of all places. He would say, "You can take the Stickymobile." I'd say "That's okay. I'll walk."

So I was young, machining parts in Wally's basement, and designing progressive stamping dies, which I'd never done. Wally would say that we had to make something that would do this or that, and I'd build it.

Wally had a sense of urgency about everything. Nothing was too meaningless. He was an early role model for me in "gettin' after it." For instance, one day he asked me to sort through a big box of junk that Virginia had bought at a yard sale and see if I could find anything useful. I was reaching in with one hand, pulling out a piece of whatever, and checking it out. He said, "No. Use two hands. It'll be faster." In a way he was like Doc in *Back to the Future*—creative, fast moving, and a little nutty.

Wally would talk about many of his other ideas, some of which had nothing to do with machines. I especially remember that he wanted to decimate the fly population of the world because he thought flies were useless.

While I was working in Wally's basement, I came up with some of my best work at the time. I also learned a great deal, from big things to small. Using whatever tools we had at hand, something I had to do as a kid with little money, was frequently how Wally approached a problem. For instance, one day we were having trouble with one of the machines we were trying to build out of scrap metal, so we drove the Stickymobile over this large piece of steel to try to bend it into place.

Wally also taught me how to combine operations. For instance, he said that you could work on the equipment and get filthy dirty hands, then could go upstairs and wash dishes. Washing the dishes would not only clean your hands and forearms, but would also clean the dishes. I thought, "Works for me, motor oil and everything."

One day Wally walked downstairs and said, "I can't pay you anymore, but you're welcome to work here." That pretty much ended my days in Wally's basement, but what I learned in those few short months has influenced me to this day.

In addition to the things I've already mentioned about efficiency, combining operations, and tackling a problem head-on, the idea that a person could make anything out of anything was profound. So-called "junk" could be turned into something productive.

On a more personal note, Wally also was the person who introduced me to health food. It was a small thing, but some mornings he would make me wheat-germ pancakes topped with real butter and real maple syrup. I'd never had either. Since then, eating well and exercising have been priorities for me.

Working with Wally also was an awakening in terms of how I viewed "old" people. At the time, I barely gave anyone who was "old" any attention and instantly devalued whoever it was. "Old, old, old" equaled no value in my young mind. What do the "old" know, anyway? At some 55 years of age, Wally was old compared to my 19 years of age, but despite my immature view of life at the time, he had tremendous value.

Chapter 3:
How Hard Could It Be?

Chapter 3:
How Hard Could It Be?

SWING OUT. TAKE A RISK.
WHAT DO YOU HAVE TO LOSE?

My Dad: Role Model?

I didn't think for the longest time that I learned anything from my dad—anything good that is. However, I realized not long ago that perhaps I did learn one useful thing from him, which can be summed up in the phrase, How hard could it be?

My parents were married for 22 years, and my dad had about 20 jobs. Some jobs he had for longer periods of time than others, and some jobs overlapped with other jobs.

My dad would get these jobs, even though he didn't have any real prior experience doing any of them. I think he figured he would simply tell whoever was hiring that he could do the job and he'd be hired sure enough. Or perhaps he just had utter faith in himself that he could do it, whatever it was.

For instance, in southern California (called "So Cal" by natives and anyone else who wants to sound cool), there was a park system that was advertising for a parks manager. My dad applied for the job and got it. How did he do that? He'd never managed a park. Similarly, along the way he said, "Of course I can manage a racehorse ranch." He got the job and we moved to the ranch and he was the manager.

In addition to working as an air traffic controller in Alaska, where he may have somehow come into possession of the helmet he let me wear, my dad had many other jobs. He was a personal pilot for a jockey. He worked at a parimutuel gambling window at Santa Anita, Corona DelMar, and Hollywood Park. He traded stocks, or at least tried to trade stocks. He was a longshoreman. He worked as a purchasing agent for a mining company. He fought forest fires. He owned two candy stores. He was a car salesman. He gave lectures on the pine forest in the Angeles National Forest. He owned a bar and grill named "Tissy's Tavern," after my mom's childhood nickname. He was the manager of one of the Cornet stores, a West-coast chain of dime stores. He worked for one of the campaigns to re-elect Jerry Pettis as a California congressman. He ran for mayor of Redlands, California, and was a member of the John Birch Society to boot.

All of these things are absolutely true. However, in addition to jobs and accomplishments that my mom or I could verify, my dad had a habit of making wild claims about his past. For example, he claimed that he raced midget cars, that he was an attaché for John Wayne, that he built a hospital in Hesperia, California, and that he flew B-17s in Germany during WWII while somehow concurrently flying in the Pacific Theater where he shot down Japanese Zeros. He also said he had flown contraband for General Manuel Noriega in Panama.

Whenever he was in the midst of one of his tales, especially one he wanted us to believe was highly important and secretive, he would say, "Oh, I can't talk about that." This was an especially convenient response when I would try to question him about these activities. Perhaps my dad's propensity for lying is one of the reasons that to this day, telling the truth is an imperative for me. Even when my kids were growing up, I never once lied to them.

My dad may have been the world's greatest fabricator about his job history and his past, but one thing's for sure: He was far from lazy. He was the hardest working person I've ever known.

Maybe I got my dad's genes for trying things out, or maybe certain things were easy for me, especially if they had anything to do with metal, connectors, and wires. And certainly Wally also had an influence on me. Or perhaps God felt sorry for me and left great opportunities sitting right in front of me and my job was to see them. Either way, all my life I've taken on many things that were seemingly beyond my skill level or too difficult because I thought, "How hard could it be?" In a practical sense, doing things that others didn't think I could do was a big plus in terms of my career.

How Hard Could It Be? 1
From Janitor to Mechanic

After I left my job in Wally's basement, I went to various machine shops looking for a job. I figured since I'd taken a three-month machine shop course at night, I could be a machinist.

One of the places I walked into was Fred G. Walter & Son, in San Bernardino. The guy who hired me handed me a broom. It was a bottom-of-the-rung job. I was a sweeper on the 4 p.m. to 5 a.m. swing shift. My job was to sweep the shop and clean out debris from the machines. It didn't bother me though because I figured I'd get in at any level and there would be nothing but upside potential.

Over time, the foreman let me clean machines they were rebuilding. Eventually I was taking things apart and rebuilding industrial-size vacuum pumps.

One day during my lunch break, I was looking at this machine called a planer. I was curious how it worked, so I fired it up. The foreman happened to walk by and yelled, "What are you doing?! Get away from there!" He screamed obscenities at me and shouted, "You don't know anything about that!"

I thought, "Yeah, I do," but I turned it off.

That didn't end my curiosity about machines, however. One of the guys who worked the night shift with me was cheating with his wife's sister. Since it was the night shift, he had to get it when he could, so he would leave, but not clock out. One night while he was gone, I decided to machine this huge shaft that was about eight feet long. The foreman caught me doing it. He asked if the other guy did it, and I said no. He said, "You did that?" I said, "Yeah, it's not really that hard."

In one sense it wasn't that hard, but I was young, 19 or 20 years old, so I guess they figured that if a young guy like me could do that, maybe I could do other things. I was soon promoted to mechanic. But I was married at the time, and she didn't like me working at night, so despite my new position with the company, I started looking for a daytime job.

How Hard Could It Be? 2
Problem Solving. Keeping It Simple

One of the places I went to look for work was a company called Rettig Machine, which was a job shop. The owners were two Germans, a father and son. I'd met them a couple of times when they had come into Carlson's Hardware looking for parts. When I applied for a job at Rettig, they said, "Oh yeah, you're that kid who used to work over at the hardware store."

My job title was something rather nondescript like "worker." I machined parts sometimes, which I had learned to do in go-karting. Other times the owners asked me to take apart machinery that they bought. I also fabricated gears and other parts and solved problems in the shop. I didn't think anything of fixing and improving things in the shop, but they began to see me as a problem solver for all kinds of issues. The foreman would say, "Come on. Let's take a ride," and we'd drive somewhere to check out a problem.

One day we took a 30-minute drive out of town into the San Bernardino Mountains. Sitting on the side of a mountain was an electrical generating station for the city's grid system. There was a huge pipe of water—about 6 to 8 feet in diameter—that ran into a concrete building. Inside the building was an impeller, essentially an enclosed water wheel, which the water ran across to spin a large shaft, which was attached to a generator, which created electricity.

The seals from the impeller to the shaft had blown, and rocks and other material from the water supply originating from the side of the mountain had severely damaged the shaft. Water had leaked everywhere. The guys at the generating station had turned the water off, but they needed to get it back online ASAP. Rettig's job was to fix the problem.

The shaft was roughly 16 inches in diameter. There was no longer any electricity to the concrete building. The generator weighed some 6 or 7 tons. And the only access to the site was via a rough, dirt road that wouldn't handle heavy equipment.

The idea was floated to build a road, break open the building, remove the generator and the damaged shaft, rig them to a semi-truck, somehow take them down the mountain, repair the shaft or attach a new one, and bring everything back up the mountain. The process was going to take weeks.

I had no idea at first why they brought me. I thought they figured we'd have to take the roof apart, try to pick up the generator and the shaft, and get it all out of the building somehow. Since I was good with cranes and picking up large objects, I assumed they viewed me as someone who might be able to help.

45

Instead, I devised a solution that fixed the whole problem, on site, in a few days. In short, we used the existing equipment to build what was essentially a lathe on the side of the mountain, and repaired the shaft better than new.

We brought in huge gears, motorcycle chain, a large air-driven mining drill like those used in the 1800s, a gas-driven generator, and an air compressor. We attached the gears to the damaged shaft, hooked one end of the chain to the gears and the other end to the teeth of the mining drill, and bolted the drill to the concrete floor of the building. The gas-driven generator powered the air compressor, which powered the drill. As a result, we were able to use this old-time mining equipment to turn the shaft.

We welded the damaged parts of the shaft as it was spinning and then machined the newly welded shaft round and smooth, so it was as good as new. The generating station was back online in about three days.

I worked at Rettig Machine for 2–3 years, but a number of dynamics had put Kaiser Steel out of business and since Kaiser was Rettig's biggest customer, this tremendously affected Rettig's business. Rettig started cutting back and cutting back and eventually I was laid off as well.

How Hard Could It Be? 3
The One-Shot Final Mold

After I was unemployed for 2–3 months, I saw an ad for a technician to set up molding machines. I'd never set up a molding machine. I'd never even seen a molding machine, but I'd set up other machines, so I thought, "How hard could it be?" The company was Tri-Tec Engineering, located at the time in Gardena, California. I was hired there as a "tool tech," which essentially meant that I set up molding machines and other wire-processing equipment. For about a year, I languished as a tool tech.

Then one day I was in my supervisor's office and I saw these things sitting on his desk. I asked what they were, and he uttered an expletive or two. I and asked if I could take them. He said, "F' you." I figured that meant I could take them, so I took them.

They were prototypes designed by one of Tri-Tec's suppliers, a company called AMP, which was the number one connector company in the world. AMP was trying to develop a new kind of connector, one that could be over-molded.

A connector is the point at the end of a cable that joins together, or connects, the wires in the cable. In order to protect the connector and the wires, a manufacturer would attach, by hand, metal or plastic covers.

The alternative was to over-mold everything by injecting hot plastic over part of the connector, wires, and cable end. Injecting hot plastic at high pressure around a connector increases its strength and durability and makes it essentially tamper proof. Molded connectors are everywhere today. Anyone who has a vacuum cleaner has seen a simple molded connector at the end of the power cord that plugs into the wall. And virtually everyone has at least more complex molded connector, one that sends and receives data, whether it's a computer cable or earphones for listening to music.

Back then, it took anywhere from 2–4 injection mold shots to create structure around the connector because connectors were not designed to be over-molded. AMP had designed a thin piece of metal that surrounded the connector wires and cable and created a metal protective suitcase of sorts. In practice, AMP created a connector that was specifically designed to be over-molded. The idea was to reduce the number of required mold shots from 2–4 to 1, thus saving a tremendous amount of manufacturing time and cost.

However, because injection molding creates a high amount of pressure, the problem was how to do it without crushing the hollow metal casing.

In one sense, who cares? However, the one-shot mold was the holy grail of cable assembly, and it had never been done. It's the kind of thing no one really hears about, but it was a big deal in industry at the time.

AMP had built some prototype connector assembles with the metal suitcase and given them to two or three other companies in the U.S, but with no success. AMP also had given Tri-Tec some prototypes, but no one at Tri-Tec was working on them. They were just sitting there on my supervisor's desk.

I figured, "How hard could it be?"

I put one of these prototypes into an injection molding machine that day. When the over-molding was complete, everything looked okay on the outside, but when I cut it apart, I realized that everything inside had been crushed and damaged. The rest of the day, I kept working on it, thinking of solutions.

I reasoned that if I could normalize the pressure around the thin outside metal by putting tiny holes in just the right places, that the pressure inside would normalize and keep the metal casing from collapsing. I came up with the idea to put four small holes in specific locations to relieve the external pressure from the molding. Sure enough, it worked.

That night, I put some samples on my supervisor's desk.

The next day, one of the owners came by and said, "Did you do this?"

I said, "Yes."

He said, "Come talk to me."

He said he had told AMP that we had done what no one else had done. Reps from AMP quickly flew out to southern California from Harrisburg, Pennsylvania, and wanted to see the results. I explained how I did it.

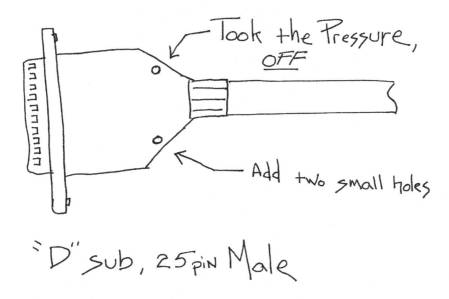

They loved my idea and thought it was clever. Later, they took it one step further, by designing miniature tabs in conjunction with the small holes. Each tab was like the tab on the top of a can of Coke. In this case, it was more like an empty can of Coke and, therefore, extremely fragile and more susceptible to collapse. As the external pressure from the injection molding built up, the tab would move slightly inside the metal suitcase, relieving the pressure.

AMP patented the design.

Before long, I was promoted from my job as "tool tech" to project leader in engineering. I designed and built cable assemblies and managed others doing the same. I began to fly around with the owners to meet with customers. We spent quite a bit of time in Silicon Valley working with start-ups such as Apple, IBM, Tandem Computers, Convergent Tech, a Tektronix affiliate, Altos (acquired by the Acer Group in 1990)—all the greats that were located in the Valley at the time.

How Hard Could It Be? 4
The Dumpster Dive

The fourth crystal-clear time in my past that I took a risk because I figured, "How hard could it be?" ended up being the catalyst for a significant turning point in my life.

One of Tri-Tec's largest customers at the time was a company in the Bay area called Tandem Computers. Tandem was one of the first companies, if not the first, to make fault-tolerant, dual-processing mini-main frames. Some guys from Tandem came to Tri-Tec and said, "You are out of control. You are unpredictable. Your lead times are too long. You need to read this book, *World-Class Manufacturing: The Lessons of Simplicity Applied*. And by the way, here's a box of them. Give them to your managers. You ought to implement the principles in this book."

The owner promptly threw the books in the dumpster after the Tandem guys left.

I wasn't in on the management meeting because I was down on the food chain, but I overheard them talking about it. I went to my engineering manager and said, "What is the deal with those books that Tandem brought?" When he told me that the owner had thrown them away, I couldn't believe it.

After work that day, I did some dumpster diving. Looking in dumpsters wasn't new for me. I had been dumpster diving ever since my mom, my brother, my sister, and I ran away from my dad and we had to fend for ourselves and live on very little money, so I had no inhibitions about going in. I found the box of books and salvaged a couple copies.

I took the books home, so I would never have them at the office. I figured if the engineering manager saw me with them, he'd fire me. Some months after I read the book, which was written by a guy named Richard J.

Schonberger, I went back to the company and said, "I have a design for a cell and I want to build one. Will you let me do it?" In short, a cell combines all of the equipment, employees, and processes in the smallest amount of space.

I told them I would create a work cell with a one-day build cycle. I would start in the morning, finish the job, and have everything on the dock that night. Completing a job in one day was a huge difference because at the time the company had a 10- to 12-week cycle time. This meant that from the moment a job was started until the time it was shipped, it was 12 weeks minimum. I said I would do it in one day.

My boss was a guy named Max. I affectionately called him BetaMax in honor of the failed, but far superior, competitor to VHS. Eventually BetaMax said, "Ok. We'll let you do it. You're on tomorrow at 7:00 a.m. How many people do you need?"

I had one day to complete this particular order. It was a job to build 200 parallel printer cables for Hewlett-Packard. I built the cell, organized the people, trained them in about 10 minutes, and we built everything in one day. We shipped 194 or 195 of the 200 cables.

Because we missed the order by 5 or 6 cables, the experiment was pronounced an abject failure by the crew. BetaMax said, "It doesn't work. It's a failure. Because you didn't hit your target, because you didn't build 200, it was a bad idea." But they didn't see the bigger picture. It shattered every convention they had in the shop.

They thought it was a failure, but I had a different perspective, which would become the basis for the business I started a couple of years later and have to this day.

A normal job at Tri-Tec took 12 weeks start to finish because of wait time at each step while other similar jobs were being completed at the same time, handling by numerous employees, as well as the physical distance the components needed to travel across the factory floor. However, for the sake of being very conservative for purposes of illustration, if there were no other jobs on the Tri-Tec factory floor, the 200 Hewlett-Packard cables would have taken some 12 days to complete.

We were able to fulfill 98 percent of the 200-cable order in one day not because I used more employees or because I used some kind of sophisticated equipment, but for one simple reason: The factory was set up to complete each *step of production* in the shortest amount of time, whereas the cell I built was set up to complete *each assembly*—the final product—in the shortest amount of time. Each employee working in the cell completed multiple tasks. In addition, the U-shaped cell took up relatively little physical floor space, approximately 10' by 3'. As a result, the cable did not have to travel far: some 23 feet (10 feet on each side of the "U" plus 3 feet), as opposed to some 700 feet if it had traveled across the factory floor.

In the work cell I designed, a cable assembly was completed approximately every 2.4 minutes. In comparison, if the assemblies had been produced using the standard mass production approach, there would have been no completed assembles until the last day, the 12th day, when all of the assemblies would have been completed at the same time.

In 1988, when I started Carrio Cabling Corporation, I used the concept of the work cell instantly, but it was a modified version of the first cell I built at Tri-Tec. From Day 1, the cell has been at the core of our manufacturing operations. Problem solving with customers at Carlson Hardware and designing and building in Wally Jones's basement were early experiences that influenced me to be sure, but the book I pulled out of the dumpster that day set the wheels in motion about the power and efficiency of the cell. In essence, you might say I retrieved my future from a dumpster.

Chapter 4:
Star Trek and the Cephloid Variable

Chapter 4:
Star Trek and the Cephloid Variable

DESIGNED SPECIFICALLY FOR YOU.
CUSTOM SOLUTIONS, SAVING TIME AND MONEY.

Star Trek's "Shore Leave"

I remember an episode of *Star Trek* I saw when I was about 10 years old. It was called "Shore Leave." It originally aired on TV a couple of years earlier. It stuck with me a long time.

In the episode, Dr. McCoy, AKA "Bones," decides that the crew needs a rest. Bones and Lieutenant Sulu beam down to an uninhabited planet to scout the site, hoping that Captain Kirk will authorize shore leave for the entire crew.

The two stroll around, looking rather happy-go-lucky. Bones contacts Kirk on his communicator and says, "You have to see this place to believe it. It's like something out of 'Alice in Wonderland.'" A few minutes later, while Sulu sets off to look around the planet, Bones encounters a large white rabbit, who pulls a gold watch from his pocket and says he's late, followed by a little girl, who looks like Alice from *Alice in Wonderland*.

Before long, Kirk, too, beams down for some rest, along with Yeoman Barrows, a beautiful, brown-hair crew member. It's quickly clear that anything the crew asks for or thinks about suddenly materializes.

Sulu thinks about an old-time police gun he always wanted and then finds one laying on the ground. Kirk recalls a guy named Finnegan, a practical joker from their days at the academy, and within moments, Finnegan is there. Their scuffles are interrupted by the screams of Yeoman Barrows, who has been attacked by Don Juan. Barrows says that she was just day-dreaming about Don Juan. Kirk runs off to look for Sulu, who is searching for Don Juan, but soon Kirk is intoxicated by some flowers; in the next moment, his long-lost love, Ruth, is standing there, looking rather intoxicating herself. And the fun continues.

Spock, of course, unlocks the key to the mysterious happenings. The crew's thoughts are being read and multi-cellular castings are being instantly manufactured by a highly sophisticated, highly evolved industrial civilization beneath the planet's surface. Apparently, the planet is a kind of amusement park for people to live out their dreams and fantasies.

The episode was classic *Star Trek*: strange goings-on; Kirk, Bones, and Sulu in some bizarre setting; and Spock logically figuring the whole thing out. I loved it for all these reasons, but I also was fascinated by the idea of instantaneously manufacturing exactly what is needed.

This idea of building something unique, to fit a specific situation, and doing it instantly stuck with me a long time. Years later, in each of my jobs, I was constantly wondering, Why does it take *so long* to make these things?

The Cephloid Custom Go-Kart Pipe

One of the first places I applied the idea of building something unique and making it instantly available was, of course, in go-karting.

Go-karting was always part of my life. No matter what job I had, I was always working on go-karts in one way or another, but I was waylaid from time to time, for various reasons, money being one of them.

Most people wouldn't choose to be poor. After all, money certainly makes life easier in many ways. But being poor can be the vehicle for creative ideas. When you can't buy something new every time you think you need it, you get creative. One of the best things I ever designed and built came about because I had no money and I wanted to be competitive in go-karts.

ALL IN THE FAMILY — Just about worth their weight in trophies, these three peppy karts are jockeyed by 10-year-old Rosie Williams, left; her 11- year-old brother Glen; and Mom (Mrs. Charles Williams) who doubles as driver and team mechanic. (Facts photos by C. J. Kenison.)

DAILY FACTS, Redlands, Calif.   Thursday, November 25, 1971 — 4

Not long after I started racing go-karts, my mom and sister, Rosie, decided to race, too. For two to three years, the three of us raced. My dad fancied himself as our manager. During this time, there was turmoil between my mom and my dad. My dad was, to put it mildly, not good to my mom, me, or Rosie. He saved whatever soft spot he had for my older brother.

Finally, my mom decided to leave and took off with Rosie. My dad put me on a plane to go live with some racing friends in Sacramento, but in order to get my mom to come back, he concocted a story, in his usual style, that I had run away. To quickly summarize this drama, my mom came back for a few months, but after a very short time, when I was about 14, she took all three of us—my sister, my brother, and me—and we ran away from my dad. For a while, we feared for our lives since my dad had threatened to kill us. He said he had employed a hit man named "Digs" because he didn't want to get his hands dirty. He told my mom not to worry, however, because he had explained to Digs not to hurt her face. We were afraid, but he had lied and threatened so many times that we were also able to laugh about it in some of our lighter moments.

Thankfully, from that day on, for the most part my dad was out of our lives for good. One of the biggest ways in which everything that happened with my dad influenced me was that I developed a profound drive to succeed and to do the right things . . . in order to prove the bastard wrong.

Sidetrack.
The Perching of Eagles:
My Near Miss with Hollywood

A month after my dad faked my run-away story, I was at an International Go-Kart Federation national championship race in Memphis, Tennessee. One of the most bizarre things that went on around that race was my debut as an actor. Thankfully, my acting career was short lived.

Apparently my dad had met a couple of guys through the gambling side of life at either the Hollywood Park or Santa Anita horse race track. They were

Hollywood producers, but they weren't "A" list producers, or even "B" or "C" list. They were more like "D" list producers (or maybe "P" list as in "porn").

He had somehow gotten these guys interested in making a film and using the novelty of our family racing together—me, my sister Rosie, and my mom—as the hook. The story was supposed to have something to do with the Mob fixing go-kart racing, and I was going to be the young star: my clear path to an Oscar. We were also told that Don Knotts was going to play the role of my dad.

About a month before the championship race in Memphis, we met with these producers in Los Angeles. It was definitely low rent. Our big meeting to discuss the movie was held at the local Motel 6.

I hadn't heard anything more since the Motel 6 gathering, so I figured the whole idea had died. But while I was at the track in Memphis practicing with the team, my dad suddenly showed up with my mom, Rosie, and a cameraman.

Before you knew it, we were filming a movie. For some unknown reason, the film was to be called *The Perching of Eagles*. The cameraman shot all kinds of scenes: scenes of racing, scenes of our family walking into the sunset on the race track, and a scene of my parents and Rosie cheering me on from the grandstands. Of course, some other guy was racing at the time, but that's beside the point.

Shortly after the film footage was shot in Memphis, my mom left my dad for good. It wasn't long before we heard the news that *The Perching of Eagles* wasn't going to happen. I think our producers failed to find enough investors or perhaps they were pitching the idea to the wrong individuals. Either way, the only remnants of my movie career are strange memories and three rusting canisters of 35mm film (how I ended up with these I don't recall), which I subsequently transferred to VHS. It's a silent movie, however, because apparently there was no budget for sound.

No Money.
Necessity Is the Mother of Invention

Sometime after that race, my dad announced that he was no longer going to pay for racing for my mom, my sister, or me. Maybe it was because *The Perching of Eagles* failed to materialize, but for whatever reason he got to the point where he didn't pay for racing anymore.

When my dad was paying for racing, we had all kinds of parts around. But when he stopped, we very quickly were out of money, out of parts, and SOL about racing. But I still wanted to race. For a long time, I borrowed exhaust pipes from racing friends, but not many guys would loan their spare pipes, so I also had a little go-kart business on the side to offset my expenses. I was working at Rettig Machine at the time and the owner said I could use any of the machines for my own purposes as long as it was after work hours. I built go-kart engines, as well as clutch rings and other parts that I could sell at the track.

Two of my closest racing buddies were Gene Day and Stuart Courtney. Like many things in life, how Gene and I met was happenstance. One day, my mom went to a full-service gas station. I'd built some go-karts, and she had them in the back of her sea-foam green Ranchero pick-up truck. While she was filling her tank, Gene came over to see the go-karts I'd built. He wanted to be a race car driver, so he bought one.

I met Stuart when I was in high school. He was working behind the counter at a go-kart shop in Ontario, California, about a 20-minute drive from my house in Redlands. One day I went by the shop to pick up something, drove home, realized I needed something else, and had to drive back.

When I walked it, I said, "It's Glen again."

Stuart said, "Hi Glen again," and that's what he tended to call me from that day on.

Stuart and I started going to various go-kart tracks to do testing. Over time, we became friends.

The three of us—Stuart, Gene, and I—became CDW, for Courtney-Day-Williams, which was still my last name at the time. We thought "CDW" sounded cool. We traveled together and worked on go-karting for a long time.

Stuart's dad was a lawyer. Stuart called him "Norm." Stuart's mom, Norm, and Stuart's sister lived in a huge house, but Stuart didn't want to live in the house, so he lived in the pool house.

Stuart's family also had a garage, where we spent many hours working on go-karting. Being a garage without much if any heat, it would get cold, even for southern California. We'd take a jumbo-size coffee can, dump racing fuel into it, throw a match on it and—WHAM!—it would light on fire, and then—WOOSH!—the floor would catch fire, too. The heat would last a long time.

Stuart was a certifiable genius. He had an IQ of something like 240 or 250. We had all kinds of great conversations. We talked about philosophy, religion, psychology, and the paranormal quite a bit. Stuart was an existentialist. He wasn't a nihilist. He hated B. F. Skinner. He thought that Jung was a moron and that Freud had his head up a dark place. We'd do primal scream therapy in Stuart's garage. He would say, "Doesn't that make you feel *good*?"

Stuart always had a Vantage Pleasure cigarette in one hand and a Dr. Pepper in the other. He'd rub the back of my neck when I'd get tense and say, "You're way too tight. You're always hung up on cause and effect. You don't understand...When you're dead, it's over!"

We also talked a lot about go-kart pipes. At the time, the exhaust pipe in go-karts was everything. It was where big horsepower and performance gains could be made. Because every race track was different, racers essentially needed a different pipe for every track. Each exhaust pipe cost between $100 and $200. Most of the guys racing at the time belonged to what Stuart, Gene, and I—CDW—affectionately called The Pipe of the Month Club. When we went to the track, there was always some new pipe. Many of our competitors had a lot of money. They could afford $250, $400 a month in pipes, whereas I couldn't.

I think it was my mother who first told me that famous line from Plato's *Republic*: "The true creator is necessity, who is the mother of our invention." I decided to build a mini pipe roller to build our own pipes. It had three rollers—two parallel rollers on the bottom and one on the top, in the middle of the other two—like three mini rolling pins. I could put a piece of sheet metal in this little machine, crank it, and rock the metal back and forth until it was rounded, and then make cones. I made the machine big enough that we banged out every imaginable size and shape. You might say it was a Zig-Zag roll-your-own for go-kart exhaust pipes.

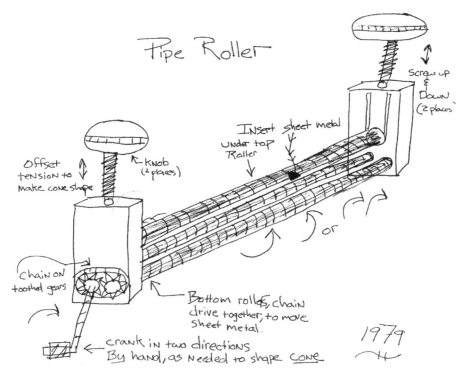

We never sold our pipes because we realized the edge it was going to give us. People would say, "Where did you get that pipe? That looks cool," but we didn't tell them.

One of the ideas we came up with was an exhaust pipe we called the Cephloid Variable. The typical go-kart exhaust pipe is a long, roundish pipe, with a cone-shaped end and a tip called a "stinger." We devised a pipe where the cone-shaped end and stinger could be easily changed or adjusted depending on how the engine ran, RPMs, top speed, the weather, and conditions at a specific track. Because the end piece, or head, looked like a cone and we could adjust its length and size, we called it the Cephloid Variable. Instead of being one complete piece, the Cephloid Variable was made of a number of detachable, adjustable parts. We built parts in different lengths and diameters that we could easily swap out.

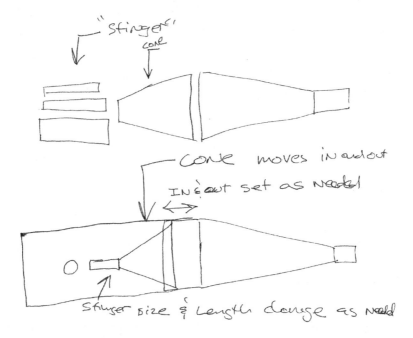

Around that time, to help reduce the noise of go-kart exhaust pipes, racing rules called for an exterior canister that had to be added over the cone and stinger end of the pipe. That new rule was a bonus for us because it made it easy for us to hide the Cephloid Variable inside a metal shell, shielding it from competitors' prying eyes.

What we came up with was unheard of at the time. Most racers had to buy a specific exhaust pipe for a specific track. They would use one pipe one time at a track, go to another track and buy another pipe, go to another track and buy another pipe, and on and on and on. As a result, most guys spent tremendous amounts of money on exhaust pipes. They had to buy seven, eight, or nine exhaust pipes during a season; with the Cephloid Variable we had *one* pipe that we could use at all kinds of different tracks.

During the testing sessions at each track, we would determine exactly what we needed to get the best performance given that particular track and the specific conditions. At the end of each test session, we would come into the pits; take out three screws, which took less than a minute; remove the exterior canister covering; lengthen or shorten the cone, attach a different size cone, or change the stinger diameter; put the screws back in; bolt and clamp it all back together; and within about two minutes, we were ready to get back on track and test it again. We'd configure it perfectly for each race track, then go to the next track and do the same thing for that track.

We didn't patent the Cephloid Variable, but it was a great idea. It affected our performance enormously from race track to track. Performance was over the top.

The point of the Cephloid Variable was that we had a single, adjustable device that was specific for our needs, could be used in multiple situations, and cut time and money. The idea of instantly making exactly what we needed—sparked by a combination of no money, an intensely competitive drive, and a dose of inspiration from *Star Trek* and my own life experiences—crystallized in the Cephloid Variable. At the time, it didn't even cross our minds that we should patent the design. We just wanted to win races. The design easily could have been patented, just as many ideas I come up with today could be patented. However, in today's manufacturing world, patenting something is counterproductive in my view, since so many overseas manufacturers have little regard for the concept of intellectual property.

Chapter 5:
Math, Equations, and Willy Wonka's Chocolate Factory

Chapter 5:

Math, Equations, and Willy Wonka's Chocolate Factory

THERE IS POWER IN SIMPLICITY.

Elementary School Math Class Distress

Like reading and writing, the third "R," 'rithmetic, frustrated me. At a simple level, I didn't understand for the longest time why these subjects were called "the three R's." My teachers would tell my parents, "He's failing the three R's." Even if I overlooked the fact that "writing" doesn't begin with an "R," I could at least make some sense of the fact that it sounds as though it ought to. The third "R," however, was bewildering since "arithmetic" starts with an "A" and "math" starts with an "M." The whole thing confused me.

Equations, in particular, were baffling. I couldn't understand them. Years later, I redeemed my near failures with math, but for all of my K–12 years, math was not only my hardest subject but the one I most despised. I was convinced that some wizened, weathered, old man sat hunched over a workbench with a vise, a chisel, and a leather mallet and worked all day to come up with math in order to torture young people. That was his sole purpose in life.

I despised math because of math itself but also because of the peripherals that went along with my numerical failings. I had no recess from 8:30 in the morning to 3:10 in the afternoon for nearly the whole of fourth grade because I hadn't learned my multiplication tables.

My teacher, Mrs. Shutt, gave me what she called a "multiplication wheel," which I was supposed to use to learn 8 x 6, 8 x 7, 8 x 8, and the rest of the times tables. I hated that wheel. Actually the wheel was simply a circle that Mrs. Shutt had drawn and then copied onto a blue ditto sheet, a term from the Dark Ages of education. There were numbers, 1 through 12, and little marks all around the wheel, like a clock. I was supposed to go clockwise around the wheel, tick by tick, and somehow learn my times tables. Day after day, all my friends went outside to recess while I was stuck inside with Mrs. Shutt and blue ditto sheets. Mrs. Shutt was bound and determined to push me through fourth grade one way or another. I'd spent two years in third grade, after failing my first go-round, and for a long time it looked like fourth grade was going to be a double header, too.

In addition to being robbed of recess time, I also was not allowed to participate in other class activities because of my math shortcomings. I especially remember the time that the school had for some reason decided to give gifts or pieces of art to the City of Redlands. I have no idea why. I just remember this "tree" of sorts in the back of our classroom. The students were to take small pieces of pink tissue paper, twist them, and then tie them onto the barren branches with thread. I think the idea was that the tree, which as I recall was really just part of a tree or a bunch of dead branches bound together, was supposed to look like it was blooming.

Since I hadn't learned my multiplication tables, I wasn't allowed to put anything on the tree. I think Mrs. Shutt viewed me as a less than full member of the class. All my classmates huddled together around this tree, twisting pieces of tissue paper and tying them on the tree, while I slaved over the times 8's. I decided it wasn't fair and set a goal to put at least one pink tissue "bloom" on the tree. One day while Mrs. Shutt was out of the room at lunch, I dashed over to the tree and tied a piece of pink tissue paper on the tree. However, consistent with my luck at that school, she came in at just the wrong moment and made me remove the twisted tissue.

Every morning before school I had a terrible stomachache. My mom thought I had an ulcer because I hated school. Her other theory was that my Superman underwear was too tight. Either way, a long way into the school year my parents finally took pity on me and intervened in the no-recess problem, saying I had to have a break and get outside.

I got back at Mrs. Shutt in the small ways I could as a kid. The first bit of revenge was the plastic snake I'd bought at Knott's Berry Farm. I put it on her desk one day by her books. As I hoped, she reached for her books, saw the snake, and screamed. The whole class laughed.

The second retaliation began, ironically, on the playground. Like every kid in every city across the United States as long as there have been schools, we weren't supposed to swing too high on the swings. Of course, like every kid since time immemorial, we did it anyway. One day several of my friends and I were in a competition to see who could swing the highest and jump off at the greatest height. I swung very high and then jumped off. I turned to walk back behind the swing to get in line to do it again. My friend had climbed onto the swing immediately after I had, swung very high, and jumped off. As he did, the swing hit me, leaving a huge cut in the side of my head. Blood was gushing everywhere.

I went back the classroom to tell Mrs. Shutt, but she was busy talking with some girls who had been in line at her desk. I tried to tell her I needed to see her right away, that I was hurt, but she told me to get back in line and wait my turn. I waited with my hand over the bloody cut. Finally, when I stood at her desk, she said rather sarcastically, "What is it you were in such a hurry to tell me?" I took my hand away from my head, which was still bleeding profusely, and, of course quite by accident, I bled all over her desk.

I did eventually make it through fourth grade. It was more of a mercy pass from Mrs. Shutt, who probably couldn't face another year of being vexed by my math inadequacies. Although I shudder a bit at the thought, I probably was an elementary school "participant."

Close-up of Ribbon "Participant" We are all winners

These are my most vivid memories about school math.

Shortly thereafter, I had an encounter with math in a completely different setting that led to a decidedly improved relationship between myself and numbers, equations, computations, and the rest of the gang. In one cool moment in the shade of a tree, I thought that perhaps these things that had for so long frustrated me might have some redeeming value after all.

Skateboarding and the $E = mc^2$ Encounter

During my elementary and middle school years, I spent a good deal of time outside on my skateboard looking for hills to test the effectiveness of different lubricants I was using in my skateboard wheels. My personal favorite, ATF, was the quickest.

Eventually I discovered a big hill by the University of Redlands, which turned out to be one of the few great racing hills near my house. One day, I was racing down one side of the hill, but thought I'd try the other side for a change. When I reached the bottom of the hill, I decided to take a break from the hot sun. Sitting in the shade at the bottom of the hill outside the university cafeteria was a small, round, low, bronze table or sculpture of some kind that had "$E = mc^2$" carved in the top.

I looked at that equation many, many times as a kid. I didn't understand it at the time, but it stuck with me. It was such a simple equation with, I later learned, tremendous power and application. Unlike the long, mind-numbing equations, diagrams, and graphs that the dashing, eloquent spaceman Klaatu finds on Professor Barnhardt's blackboards in the great movie *The Day the Earth Stood Still*, which I'd seen years earlier, $E = mc^2$ was simple and powerful.

Operator Rate Per Conductor

Someone once said that all things can be expressed mathematically. While I was working at Tri-Tec Engineering, I came up with a simple, but useful equation—Operator Rate Per Conductor—that was the precursor to one of the most valuable concepts I use in business today.

All of the equipment manufacturers we dealt with at Tri-Tech made claims about how great their equipment was, but their advertised capabilities were expressed in different ways. I was looking for a way to put these capabilities on a par, so I could more accurately compare them.

I used the smallest unit in cable assembly, a wire, more technically referred to as a *conductor*, to create a simple concept: Operator Rate per Conductor, or ORPC. When an employee—an operator—builds a cable assembly, he or she handles each conductor in the assembly. Expressing production in terms of the number of assemblies produced per hour, or number of assemblies produced per hour per operator is useful; however, knowing the ORPC—how quickly an operator can process a conductor—is valuable because a cable assembly might have 1 conductor or 100 conductors. How fast can one operator process one conductor? Said another way, what is the cycle time of one conductor? Using ORPC, every piece of equipment, and every manufacturing process involving cables, can be compared in terms of how fast one conductor can be processed.

The value of calculating ORPC is that it results in tangible units of measurement to test against, to calculate the relative efficiency of machines and various production lines. I used ORPC when I visited other factories or considered purchasing equipment, but one of the first places I applied it was Tri-Tec's "D-sub" cable assembly line.

Tri-Tec had a 12-person mass production line that built D-sub cable assemblies, which is a common electronic connector so named because it is, quite simply, shaped like the letter "D." The D-sub line produced stacks of assemblies every day, however, management wanted even more output from the line. Their solution was to add more employees to the line and break down the production tasks even further. They asked me to find a way to improve the productivity of the line.

I determined that, when viewed as a total unit, the D-sub line was highly inefficient compared to other pieces of equipment and production processes Tri-Tech was using. For instance, the D-sub line was 40 percent less efficient than a cable assembly machine we used called a Champ-o-Mator. (As a side note, years later, the hyphens were dropped and it became the Champomator, but the original Champ-o-Mator was available at the same time as the Amp-o-Lectric and the Amp-o-Matic. I think all of these products were inspired by Ronco's Veg-o-Matic and other "o-Matic" products, which *Saturday Night Live* later parodied in two classic episodes featuring Dan Aykroyd and the Super Bass-o-Matic and the Super Bat-o-Matic.)

To put it in simple terms, each D-sub cable assembly had 37 conductors, which were handled twice—on each end of the cable—for a total of 74 conductors per assembly. The Champ-o-Mator put out 10 cable assemblies per hour, which meant that 740 conductors were processed each hour. By comparison, Tri-Tec's D-sub line had an output of 72 cable assemblies per hour, or 5,328 conductors (72 x 74) each hour.

On the surface, the D-sub line looked infinitely better than the Champ-o-Mator: 5,328 conductors versus 740 conductors. However, 12 employees were needed to run the D-sub line, whereas only one employee was needed to run the Champ-o-Mator. As Exhibit 1 shows, the Champ-o-Mator was much more efficient in every way compared to the D-sub production line. The Champ-o-Mator processed a conductor every 4.86 seconds, a rate some 40 percent more efficient than the D-sub line's 8.11 seconds.

Exhibit 1. Champ-o-Mator Production

	# of Cable Assemblies per Hour	# of Conductors per Hour	Required Number of Operators	# of Conductors per Hour per Operator	OPRC (in seconds)
D-sub Line	72	5,328 (72 x 74)	12	444 (5,328 ÷ 12)	8.11 (3600÷444)
Champ-o-Mator	10	740 (10 x 74)	1	740 (740÷1)	4.86 (3600÷740)

It was apparent to me that the problem was the 12-person D-sub production line itself. There were inefficiencies everywhere. For instance, the job of the man at the beginning of the line was to take the precut cable off the rack, strip the two ends, and hand it to the first of several color coders. The cable stripper could work at a very high rate of production, but the employee who was the first color coder was much slower, so the cable stripper slowed down to match the color coder's speed. A similar situation occurred at the end of the line. When the cable assembly was finished, the tester would pick up the assembly, plug it into an electronic testing device, scan it for "pass" or "fail," unplug it, and put it on a rack. The tester could run at a high production rate, but like the cable stripper at the beginning of the line, the tester slowed his rate to match the rate of the person before him on the line. The overall effect of these differences was that the line assumed the lowest rate of production.

I was beginning to see the manufacturing world more and more in terms of the incredible efficiency of the work cell compared to the production line.

It was clear to me that the raw output of the 12-person D-sub production line was impressive, but it was inherently inefficient and inflexible because it could only process a certain type of wire. My recommendation was to break up the line and create 12 individual, independent work stations—work cells—where each person would perform all of the tasks and build complete cable assemblies. However, management did not see how the change would equate to increased output of D-sub assembles. I think they were so impressed by the large racks of cable assemblies that the line produced in one location and, like so many companies today, so mesmerized by mass production that they simply could not make the mental shift.

Willy Wonka and One Operator = ™

The frenzy of mass production and the apparently irresistible urge companies have to break every manufacturing process down to highly discrete tasks—driven by the assumption that if we break down tasks, we can work faster—are wonderfully exemplified in the 2005 movie *Charlie and the Chocolate Factory*. One of my favorite scenes takes place in the round, white-and-blue room of Willy Wonka's factory where dozens of trained squirrels are shelling walnuts, as squirrels do. These squirrels are essentially nut quality inspectors. Each squirrel grasps a walnut and cracks it open. If the squirrel thinks it might be a bad nut, he taps it and then puts it to his ear to listen. If indeed it is a bad nut, he throws it over his shoulder and the nut rolls down the tapered floor, falling through a hole in the middle of the room to an incinerator below. No one is supposed to go into the room because these are trained squirrels.

Fortunately, the squirrels in Wonka's factory work very fast. But what if they didn't? They might easily end up like Lucy and Ethel in the famous scene from *I Love Lucy* that shows the two working in the wrapping department of a chocolate candy factory. The conveyor belt moves the chocolates along at a reasonable speed, but before long it is going faster and faster and faster. To keep up and make sure there are no piles of chocolates when the boss returns, Lucy and Ethel start eating the chocolates.

One wonders what happens to the shelled walnuts in Willy's factory after the squirrels are finished with them. Are the Oompa Loompas as fast as the squirrels are? Are they able to keep up with the piles of shelled walnuts? Or do they face growing mounds of nuts?

The squirrel scene is a great example of the mass production mentality. The squirrels only shell the walnuts and dispose of rejects. But why not have them do more than one job? In addition to shelling each walnut, the squirrels could hand-dip the shelled nut in chocolate, wrap it in plastic, put the dipped nut in a box, and wrap the box with a bow, ready for shipping. These squirrels could easily do more, couldn't they? After all, they are highly trained squirrels.

Over time, I realized that there was an even simpler, and more powerful, equation for determining the relative efficiency of *all* manufacturing operations. In conjunction with Operator Rate Per Conductor, I developed One Operator =™. All manufacturing operations—scheduling, quoting, planning, machine output, and so on—can be expressed in terms of the production of one employee, or one operator.

For purposes of highlighting the relative advantages of a work cell over the typical mass production line—and using One Operator =™ as the backdrop—let's assume that a group of squirrels are working in Willy Wonka's factory making delectable, nutritious chocolate-dipped walnuts.

Question: In the ordinary world of mass production, how many squirrels does it take to produce one delicious, out-of-this world, chocolate-dipped walnut?

Answer: Four.

> One to crack open and inspect the walnut
>
> A second to dip the nut in chocolate
>
> A third to wrap the dipped nut in plastic
>
> A fourth to inspect the dipped nut, put it in a box, and wrap the
> box with a bow, ready for shipping

Now let's assume that each of the four squirrels has attended intensive employee training for nut cracking and inspection, nut dipping, nut wrapping, and nut final inspection and packing. In reality, squirrel #1 takes 8 seconds to complete its task; squirrel #2, 6 seconds; squirrel #3, 12 seconds; and squirrel #4, 30 seconds, resulting in numerous additional problems related to accumulated piles, of varying sizes, of inspected, dipped, and wrapped nuts, waiting for final inspection and packing. This is the problem every manufacturer creates when he or she uses the highly wasteful work-in-process, mindless approach to mass production.

However, to keep that aspect of mass production out of the picture for the moment, let's assume that each squirrel completes its task in 10 seconds. As Exhibit 2 shows, the combined tasks of the four squirrels total 40 seconds of labor time to process one chocolate-dipped walnut, wrapped in plastic, and placed in a box, ready for shipping.

Exhibit 2. Nut Production Line

Squirrel	Task	Labor Time
#1	Cracks open & inspects the walnut	10 seconds
#2	Dips the nut in chocolate	10 seconds
#3	Wraps the dipped nut in plastic	10 seconds
#4	Inspects the dipped, wrapped nut for quality; puts it in a box; and wraps the box with a bow, ready for shipping	10 seconds
	Total	**40 seconds**
	Nut Production Per Hour	**360 nuts**

After the production line is up and running, the line will produce 360 completed nuts per hour—one every 10 seconds.

Now let's assume that, in place of the Nut Production Line, Willy decides to revamp his chocolate factory and create Squirrel Cells. As shown in Exhibit 3, a Squirrel Cell consists of one squirrel that has been cross-trained to perform all of the tasks of inspecting, shelling, dipping, wrapping, and packing each nut, preparing it for shipment. The squirrel is able to produce one delicious, nutritious, chocolate-dipped walnut, wrapped and ready for shipping every 30 seconds.

Exhibit 3. Squirrel Cell

Squirrel	Tasks	Labor Time
Squirrel #1	Cracks open & inspects the walnut	
	Dips the nut in chocolate	
	Wraps the dipped nut in plastic	
	Inspects the dipped, wrapped nut for quality; puts it in a box; and wraps the box with a bow, ready for shipping	
	Total	**30 seconds**
	Nut Production Per Hour	**120 nuts**

Now let's compare the output of the Nut Production Line with that of one Squirrel Cell, shall we? The Nut Production Line produces 360 delicious, ready-to-ship, chocolate-dipped walnuts each hour. The Squirrel Cell, on the other hand, produces 120 delicious, ready-to-ship, chocolate-dipped walnuts every hour. On the surface, there's no comparison; 360 is clearly better than 120. However, when we apply One Operator =™, or in this case, One Squirrel =™, we get an entirely different view:

Nut Production Line: One Squirrel = 90 (360/4)
Squirrel Cell: One Squirrel = 120 (120/1)

It's not complicated. The Nut Production Line uses four squirrels. The Squirrel Cell requires only one squirrel. Since *one* Squirrel Cell produces 120 completed nuts every hour, *three* squirrels working in independent Squirrel Cells produce 360 nuts every hour: the same number of delicious, ready-to-ship, chocolate-dipped walnuts that *four* squirrels produce on the Nut Production Line. In short, the cell approach to nut production is 25 percent more efficient than the production line. The reason that one squirrel working in a Squirrel Cell completes the tasks more efficiently is simple: There is no handoff of the nut to another squirrel at each stage of production, and less likelihood of error due to miscommunication, both of which translate into significant savings in labor time.

The mass production mentality of breaking down a job into discrete tasks and putting many employees to work on the job leads to tremendous inefficiencies, to say nothing of repetitive motion injuries and, in this case, increased dental expenses due to chipped squirrel teeth. In addition, the squirrels on the Nut Production Line are likely to have low morale, high absenteeism, hypertension, and high anxiety. After all, everyone knows that squirrels are smart, and the boring, repetitive nature of life on the assembly line is more than they can take. They, quite literally, are likely to go nuts.

On the other hand, the squirrels working in independent work cells are likely to have a higher sense of pride in accomplishing their tasks, more ownership of the production process start to finish, and be significantly more challenged and engaged in their work. Countless times, I have noticed the healthy competitive spirit among employees who are given the opportunity to be challenged, independent, and truly own their work.

How does all of this apply to business? Simple. U.S. manufacturers can never compete with offshore outsourcers on pure price given currency manipulations, government subsidies, and material substitutions, which are frequently made willy-nilly by overseas companies. Nor can we compete on labor cost alone. However, when other critical factors are considered— lower cycle and delivery times, zero defects, lower transportation costs, lower minimum quantities, and the ability to rapidly change specifications—U.S. manufacturers beat overseas manufacturers hands down.

The cellular approach to manufacturing is the key to many of these benefits and instantly puts a company at a competitive advantage in the marketplace.

If you don't see how this applies to your particular company or your life, here are a couple of everyday examples to ponder of the mindless, wasteful mass production approach to just about anything. What's wrong with all of us? Why are we driven to divide our tasks into discrete components and act like mindless robots? These examples remind me of the joke, "How many lawyers does it take to screw in a light bulb?"

Ordering a Burrito at Your Local Fast Food Restaurant

You know the drill. One employee takes your order and your slowly growing burrito is pushed down the line from employee to employee to employee. If you're lucky and have enough time, you'll get your burrito the way you wanted it and before the beans taste like dried-up Elmer's glue.

Employee #1: "May I take your order?"

You: "Yes. I'd like a chicken burrito with black beans, guacamole, light cheese, and mild sauce."

Employee #1: *No response. Employee #1 puts your flour tortilla in the tortilla steamer, and then takes the order of the next customer in line.*

Employee #2: *Takes your hot flour tortilla out of the steamer and asks,* "What do you want on your burrito?"

You: "Ok....I'll have chicken with black beans, guacamole, light cheese, and mild sauce."

Employee #2: *No response, but Employee #2 puts chicken on your flour tortilla and pushes it down the counter to Employee #3.*

Employee #3: "What do you want on your burrito?"

You: (*noting that the chicken is already on the tortilla*) "I'll have black beans, guacamole, a little cheese, and mild sauce.... Oh, and lettuce."

Employee #3: *Puts black beans, guacamole, and a little cheese on your tortilla, and pushes your quickly cooling burrito down the counter to Employee #4.*

Employee #4: *Blank stare.*

You: (*noting that black beans, guacamole, and a little cheese are now on the tortilla*) "I'll have mild sauce and lettuce."

Getting a Refund From Any Company

Why does it take six or eight weeks to get a refund check from your phone company, insurance company, credit card company—really, any company? I recently had an interaction with a credit card company that is a perfect example of the amazing amount of time that so many tasks seem to take in our supposedly high-tech, highly effective world. Does this sound familiar?

A credit card company charged me interest and additional charges totaling some $19.06 because I supposedly didn't pay the balance on time. I had contested the balance earlier, after noticing that the charges on my bill were charges I had not made. After two months of haggling over $19.06, I decided to just pay the $19.06 because it simply wasn't worth my time anymore. The credit card company eventually deleted the charges and decided to refund me the $19.06, but it took another two months for them to get me a refund check. Of course, along the way I spoke with no less than five people about the $19.06 in charges. Now, how much time did it actually take to do the work involved? Five minutes? Ten minutes? Thirty minutes? Certainly far less than 60 days. Let's not even get into the labor charges wasted by these five people, to say nothing of the value of everyone's time.

. . . .

I could go on and on, and give example after example in every field, from so-called fast food to auto-body repair to plumbing a bathroom to the printing of custom t-shirts to manufacturing plastic water bottles. In every case, the cellular, One Operator $=^{TM}$ approach can equate to labor efficiencies, reductions in warranty expenses, and gains in employee satisfaction, to name just a few of the benefits to owners. As the customer, you will get whatever it is—your sandwich, product, part, paperwork, refund check, etc.—much more quickly, not twice, three times, or ten times as long as necessary. And the quality, accuracy, thoroughness—in other words, all of the details of any manufacturing or business process—are always better, no question about it. Sounds too good to be true, doesn't it?

Chapter 6:

Campfire Stories from the Business Asylum

Chapter 6:

Campfire Stories from the Business Asylum

BE CLEAR ABOUT YOUR CORE PRINCIPLES AND STICK TO THEM.

Why Cables? The Accidental Manufacturer

How I ended up manufacturing cables was somewhat by happenstance, somewhat because I kept doing what others didn't think I could do, and perhaps somewhat by luck or God's grace. One thing seemed to lead to another, from selling hardware to sweeping floors to machining to engineering...and then making cables. I was inspired along the way by a number of things, primarily *Star Trek*'s "Shore Leave," Wally Jones, and a book I retrieved from a dumpster. In a way, I became an accidental manufacturer, building connectors, cables, and coil cords, one at a time, designed specifically for each customer, in real time, and delivered now.

Most days at Carrio Cabling the work and risk are worth the ultimate rewards, but some days I'm not so sure. It's those days that my resolve to stay on point, stay focused, and stay true to my principles is tested.

You Didn't Order This, But You'll Take It

For instance, one day . . .

A few years ago, 35,000 feet of cable showed up on our dock from a large manufacturing company, one that gained a great deal of media coverage for its unethical business practices. The company became infamous for the millions of dollars it gave to its CEO to purchase a mansion and all kinds of luxury items that had nothing to do with running a business.

We hadn't ordered this cable, and there was no agreement of any kind with this company to ship us the cable. It just showed up.

We called the company and said, "Apparently you've made a mistake. This cable showed up and we didn't order it. We'll help you get it on a truck and send it to whatever customer was supposed to get it because it's certainly not for us since Carrio doesn't accept anything unless we've issued a purchase order for it."

Their response: "Well, can't you use it?"

"We've used it in the past, and maybe over a year or more we could use it, but we don't need it now and we didn't order it."

Their response: "We're not taking it back."

Again, Carrio Cabling had no purchase order for this cable, and there was no contractual agreement of any kind with this company to purchase it. This company had just arbitrarily shipped some 35,000 feet of cable to us, which at approximately $.50 a foot was some $17,500 worth of cable they delivered to our dock and said, "Well, can't you use it?"

There are days where it's hard to keep my composure, and this was one of them.

"Do you expect me to eat nearly 18 grand? We're shipping it back."

"No you're not."

"The hell we're not."

I instructed my people to ship it back immediately.

They somehow stopped the shipment halfway, called us, and said, "We need to negotiate this."

"Negotiate what? I never bought it. There's no dispute. It's not like it's a misunderstanding. If we had ordered it, we would pay for it, but we didn't order it and we don't need it."

Everyone acknowledged that Carrio Cabling did not order it, but apparently that didn't matter. This company tried to force us to buy something we didn't order and didn't want.

"You're going to take this cable," the guy said.

We fought with this company for more than six months. They jumped all over us about cable we never ordered and sent us late notices that we were past due on $17,500 worth of cable. To add insult to injury, they also tried to tack on shipping charges, again, for cable we didn't order.

Back-Dating Purchase Orders

But wait, there's more. Another time . . .

One of the most insidious tricks that another company used for many years—a highly visible, multinational conglomerate—was back-dating purchase orders and then blasting Carrio Cabling as a supplier for being "late." This company has various ways in which it grades its suppliers, one of which is the extent to which the supplier delivers on time.

A couple of years ago, our company contacts told us we were late something like 30 percent of the time and because we were so "late," we weren't a very good supplier. Further, because they had decided we weren't a good supplier, we had to lower our price. They wanted to know what kind of corrective action we were going to take to be a better supplier. My response: "We're going to do nothing."

Back-dating purchase orders many months or years in the past is one of this company's most underhanded schemes. They use it to try to keep a supplier in the lowest possible position.

For instance, we would receive a purchase order from this company on, say, October 15, 2006, that noted the due date as December 2, 2004, two years earlier. It was not a typo because they did this kind of thing over and over and over again.

We would call and say, "You might not have noticed, but there's a mistake on your purchase order." They wouldn't acknowledge that there was a mistake and wouldn't change it. We had worked with this company a long time at that point, so we built what they requested because clearly they needed it. However, apparently no good deed goes unpunished.

Fortunately at Carrio Cabling, we keep track of our real delivery dates. As a result, we have highly specific information about every one of our shipments and can track when each was shipped, when it arrived, who signed for it, etcetera. We know for a fact that since 2004, Carrio Cabling's on-time delivery rate has been at least 97.18 percent. In other words, we are late, at most, 2.82 percent of the time.

But this company said, "You are late 30 percent of the time." I don't know what kind of fool they thought I was. And then they had the audacity to call and write demanding letters, "What corrective action are you going to take to avoid this?" It was unbelievably absurd.

Online Auctions:
Etch A Sketch and Middle School Bullies

And then there was the day . . .

There is a poorly conceived and poorly executed business fad that hopefully is dying out called online auctions. The company we dealt with was essentially a modern-day auctioneer. Tyco and other companies go to this company, which is supposed to get massive cost reductions for Tyco and the rest of the gang. In our case, there were some 200 different types of cable assemlies we were supposed to bid on, which sounded clear enough, but that's where the clarity ended.

The first hurdle was the statement of terms and conditions we were required to sign to get a bid number and a package. We accepted the terms within a couple of days of being notified about this process. When we finally received the package, there was a statement that the time for questions was between August 1 and August 8. The company, of course, delivered the package to us on August 28.

We called them dozens of times, but could never get through to anyone.

There are so many problems with this fad of online auctioneering, but the one that is the most ridiculous is the Etch A Sketch nature of the diagrams that a company is supposed to use for bidding. Pages were missing, dimensions were missing, and many of the pages looked like copies of faxed copies of faxed copies of faxed copies, like some bizarre connect-the-dots game of "Guess what this is?"

"I think that's an arrow."
"Looks more like an arrowhead."
"Is that a number 1?"
"I think so, but it could be a 4."

And the fun continued.

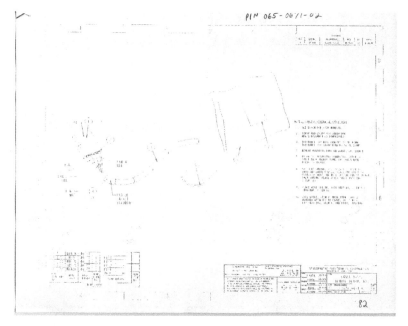

Apparently we needed to hire some kind of cable swami or sign up for a mind-reading class to figure out what the drawing was.

Another version of "Guess what?" cable divination was the digital picture we received of a piece of wire with a couple of ends on it.

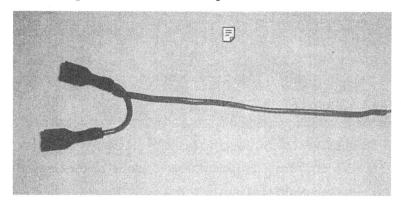

We were supposed to quote this thing at 10,000 units a year. But that's all the information we received. A picture of a piece of wire. Is the picture to scale? Is it actual size? Or fun size? How long is it? How wide is it? Where does it go? What color is it? How will it be used? We finally reached someone at the company, but the answer to all of our answers was no response other than, "Are you going to bid on this or not?"

Now mind you, we'd been warned that if they didn't like how we dealt with them, they would put us "in the penalty box," and hurt us in the bidding process or that we would "not get out of the gates in this horserace." Truly middle school stuff.

I finally said, "No thanks," to which the contact responded, "You must bid on this, or you will be blacklisted." I said, "Ok, fine. Everything is $100."

Their response: "You can't bid that number. It's not a realistic bid."

To which I replied, "Actually, it *is* realistic because I have no idea what this stuff is. Your diagrams are barely discernable, information is missing, pages are missing. So, fine, put me on your stupid blacklist."

The companies that win in this ridiculous system must be companies that throw out a near-zero number, a number so incredibly low that they are sure to win. Then when they get the actual dimensions, they put in a real bid and claim they didn't know what the product was in the first place or that prices on raw materials have increased. Or perhaps what really goes on is that that some prize vendor has already been awarded the entire package and the whole thing is a ruse to prove that the auctioneer and its customer have received other bids.

Supplier Appreciation Day

The ultimate, the pinnacle of bad business behavior was the day . . .

The coup de grâce was "Supplier Appreciation Day."

Several years ago, one of our major customers at the time—an extremely visible company in today's world—held what it called "Supplier Appreciation Day." Sounds simple and straightforward enough, yes? Wrong.

I flew out to the company's headquarters. I met with a number of people, including the buyer we'd been dealing with for years, in a large conference room at a nearby hotel. Eventually I was assigned to a smaller room. There were three individuals in the room, none of whom I knew. One of the individuals was a woman I'll call "Beatrix." Some guy closed the door. A third person was standing in front of the door like a goon or a bouncer at a bar.

We sat down at the table and Beatrix said, "Here's the deal. Here are the prices you are going to sell us these things for. And by the way, if you don't sign this contract, you are going to lose all the business. Better still, you are not leaving this room until you sign this contract."

I made a few jokes, figuring this was some kind of amusing way to start the meeting, but no one laughed.

I uttered an expletive, roughly translated as "no way," and said, "You've got to be kidding me? What are you going to do if I don't sign? Is Joe Bouncer here going to take out a small-caliber pistol and shoot me in the kneecaps?" No one answered. No one smiled. I uttered another expletive, stood up, and walked out. As I left, Beatrix said, "That's the dumbest thing you could ever do."

I got in my car, drove to the company's headquarters, and tried to reach the buyer by phone. He couldn't be reached, so I left him a message. "I've been given an ultimatum to lower my prices or lose the business. I will not be threatened or coerced. Even though you are basically throwing us out as a supplier, I will give you the same price that we have been giving you so far. I will uphold that price until you find your new supplier. I'll give you the same delivery terms, the same quality, the same packaging—everything that you know and love about us today. All I ask is that you give me the cutoff day so I don't get stuck holding additional materials and that way I can wind your product down, but I won't shut your lines down. And oh, by the way, here are the names of three of my competitors if you'd like to talk with them."

I got on a plane that afternoon and flew back home. I sold all of my stock in the company the next day.

We did a booming business with this company for years after that, but I never attended another "Supplier Appreciation Day."

Outside the Land of Logic in the Nutty World of Price

Every day at Carrio Cabling, something crazy happens about price. I could relay 100s of stories about the nutty view companies have about price. For now, here are two snippets. Before you read these, throw out all those math formulas you learned in school, not just the ones you learned in college but the ones you learned in third grade. Life as we know it is not the same here.

Scenario #1

4 cents > 30 cents
4 cents > $500.30

One of our customers is a medical supply company that manufacturers a device that moves up and down as the medical technician uses it.

Customer: "We're having trouble with warranties. The plastic tie wraps that hold together cables you make are cutting the cables as the device moves."

Carrio: "We can build you a clamp that will hold the cables firm and eliminate the need for tie wraps. And we'll build it for free."

Months later.

Carrio: "Do you want us to build the clamps for you? We can ship them tomorrow."

Customer: "No. They're going to cost more."

Carrio: "We said we would build them at no cost."

Customer: "I know, but each clamp requires 4 screws in order to mount it. Each screw costs 1 cent each, so that means we will have to spend 4 cents more per piece of equipment."

Carrio: "Yes, but you'll save 30 cents in materials alone for every piece of equipment and well over $500 per when you consider warranty savings."

Customer: "But each one is going to cost 4 cents more."

Not long after this exchange, Carrio Cabling received a letter from the company stating that we needed to lower our prices by 6% per quarter, so that inside of 3 quarters we would be down by 18%. We could have lowered the customer's prices in other ways, including the recommendation we made on the cable clamps as well as other design improvements we suggested over the years, but it's simpler to ask the supplier to cut prices.

Scenario #2:

Cost does not include shipping costs.
And it's a good idea to order thousands more than needed and wait months so that you can get a lower per-unit price.

A company contacted us and said they needed 250 cable assemblies. The product was being phased out, so the company only needed 250 assemblies, but absolutely had to have them "yesterday."

A day or two later, we sent them a quote. Eventually a company buyer called to say that our price was too high because they could get the assemblies in China for half the price. Now mind you, they wanted to know if we could build them ASAP, because, again, they had to have them "yesterday." They complained about the Chinese company's long lead time of some four months and huge minimum order of 3,000 assemblies. They then asked if we could build the assemblies but not build them according to UL/CSA standards, a sure lawsuit. Obviously we said no.

I believe they ultimately chose to buy 3,000 assemblies from China—2,750 of which they didn't need—for a higher total price, plus substantially higher shipping costs. But apparently none of that mattered. You would think it was dead-easy math, but they wouldn't do it. They were fixated over the per-assembly price, rather than taking into consideration the total cost of delayed delivery time, uncertain materials, and no safety standards. I estimate that they spent an extra $10,000 for 250 cable assemblies.

Other Snippets from the Asylum

I could fill an entire book with more instances of unbelievable, but true, practices I have experienced firsthand working with companies in today's business environment. For now, I'll end this chapter with just a few additional highlights.

• A well-known, major company decided to raise its prices. Carrio Cabling had a purchase order with the company for a specific price, and we had paid all of our bills to date. The new price went into effect now, our rep said, but it also applied to everything we had already paid for under this purchase order. In essence, it was a price increase in arrears.

• Another company, already discussed in this book, takes Carrio's 3 percent/net 10 discount, even though they consistently pay 30–90 days past the due date.

• Another company told us, "In order to deal with us, you have to give us your raw costs in advance, and we'll tell you how much profit you are going to make." Think about it. If a company's margin is, say, 10 percent, as a supplier I'm supposed to be blessed with .1 percent profit. Oh, that's right—I guess that's what's meant by a "win-win" situation.

• One day, I received a voice mail message from someone who sounded quite distressed. She had apparently already spoken with Richard, Carrio Cabling's chief financial officer, and couldn't be more displeased with him, with me, and with Carrio Cabling. Approximately a year prior to that time, we had purchased, paid for, and used an online employee aptitude test offered by her company, an allegedly first-rate Colorado company. We completed our agreement and paid all of our bills in full, but there had been a downturn in the economy and we decided to no longer purchase the service. She was irate. "Richard told me you don't need our product anymore," she yelled into my voice mail. "I want to know why you aren't buying this from us!"

I received a similar message from someone who worked for a company that made labels. We had purchased labels from this company, but decided to purchase the same labels from another supplier at a better price with much better customer service. When I returned her call, she couldn't have been more nasty, rude, and angry.

You're right, I can't wait to buy more product from companies that employ sales people with this kind of attitude. Perhaps using irate customer service personnel is some kind of new sales tool, designed to appeal to someone; I just don't know who.

Chapter 7:
Still Yenning for China Made:
The Quest for Near-Zero Pricing

Chapter 7:
Still Yenning for China Made: The Quest for Near-Zero Pricing

I've saved my favorite topic for the last chapter of this book:

The quest for near-zero pricing and our continuing infatuation with "made in China"

The quest for near-zero pricing, the most revered of quests for many companies, is symbiotically linked with American consumers' desire for lower and lower prices, shareholders' desire for higher and higher gains, and the continuing acceptance of products made in China, even those that are clearly substandard. Witness the growth of Wal-Mart, a mega-store that stocks its shelves with low-priced—and in many cases low-quality—items, the vast majority of which are made in China.

The problem with products made in China is that many of them are deficient, defective, poor quality, or downright dangerous in some way.

Let's stop right there for a minute.

Anyone who talks about the made-in-China topic is instantly labeled as some kind of racist. It's an easy thing to say in this day of politically correct speech. The problem is that the questionable quality of China-made goods has zero to do with race or ethnicity. In fact, American business executives—White, Black, periwinkle, magenta—who are willing to accept substandard products in the quest for prices as close to zero as possible are perhaps equally to blame, if we're looking to assign blame.

Let's review just a few of the made-in-China consumer product tales so familiar to us. Lead paint on children's toys. Poisonous dog food. Toothpaste tainted with an industrial solvent used in anti-freeze. Tires missing a critical safety feature. Seafood laced with potentially dangerous antibiotics.

In the manufacturing world, the issue is just as big a problem. For instance, in cable assembly and connector manufacturing, I have personally disassembled and examined China-made cable assemblies that fall well below any standard of quality:

- Copper in cables that isn't really copper
- Gold that isn't really gold
- Products labeled as UL compliant or ISO accreditation that aren't
- Cable assemblies that are required by specification to include flame retardant, but don't

The variance between American-made goods—or for that matter, products made in any number of other countries—and those made in China is remarkable. Whose fault is it? One or more of the following is likely occurring:

- The Chinese company takes leeway in material substitutions and manufacturing processes without telling the American company.
- The Chinese company takes leeway and tells the American company, but the American company looks the other way. "The Chinese company said it has met the specifications. That's good enough for us."
- The American company actually lowers its quality standards when it sends business to China, while holding American suppliers to a

higher standard. If my company built a product according to these lower standards, we'd be sued.

It matters little whether it's the American manufacturer's fault or the fault of the Chinese company. The result is the same: The list of products made in China that are defective, unsafe, or plain do not work goes on and on and on.

Yet, American companies continue to send their business to China. The reason? The insatiable quest for lower and lower and lower prices until we reach zero.

When I started Carrio Cabling 25 years ago, price mattered. You can't be in business and not care about price. But the focus on fair pricing was always coupled, until recently, with a focus on quality and delivery. It was a given: Of course, quality and delivery mattered. Today, what matters to 90% of businesses is the purchase price, pure and simple.

The following viewpoints and priorities seem to be the guide:

1. Price is the #1, #2, and #3 priority. Quality and delivery are virtually irrelevant. What matters is price.

2. There is a willingness to pay a great deal for delivery, accept very long delivery times, and incur increased warranties and customer returns as long as the price for the item itself is low. Potential lawsuits due to faulty materials or poor quality are not the priority they were years ago, as long as the price is low. This attitude is often closely linked to a willingness to buy many more items than needed so that price for each item is lower.

3. Manufacturing in China is best for consumers, manufacturers, financial services, food processing—every sector of our economy— because it's cheap.

4. Because manufacturing prices from China are so low, prices offered by American manufacturers must go down . . . and down . . . and down, until they reach near-zero. However, these cost reductions are frequently not passed on to consumers. At the consumer level, retail prices decrease very little, if at all.

5. The ability to discern seems to have disappeared. For instance, if a supplier says a product has gold or copper on its cables, then it's gold or copper even though the "gold" looks more like gold crayon and the "copper" is really an amalgam of unknown materials with very little actual copper. What matters is price, pure and simple.

As companies attempt to get lower and lower prices, they grind their suppliers on price. Is it any wonder that there are quality problems in the marketplace today? As suppliers are ground down more and more and more, some of these companies will make material substitutions or cut corners that result in problems ranging from simple, low-impact problems (for instance, a product that can be used 1 or 2 times before breaking) to dramatic, potentially dangerous problems with high impacts on everyone.

Companies that do business like this overlook shipping costs, delays, high minimum-order requirements, warehousing requirements, warranty problems, possible litigation if the product fails, and lost American jobs, all for the goal of reduced costs and higher profits.

Unfortunately, American companies simply cannot compete with "half price"—or lower—China pricing. Nearly every day, I get a call or email from a company that wants Carrio quality at China prices. Our prices are very competitive compared to a normal company in the U.S. But when the China price is less than the cost of our materials alone, obviously there is no way to compete if, again, price is truly the only factor.

The only bright light is that ultimately quality does matter to many companies; and when they get burned by offshore manufacturers, they do come back to the United States. Unfortunately, they are still hung up in the mentality of near-zero pricing.

So what's a business owner to do?

If business is only about money, then all American companies should close today, relocate to the place with the cheapest labor, the cheapest materials, and the cheapest everything—likely somewhere outside the United States: China, Vietnam, India, or the latest emerging low-cost country—find workers to exploit, and open up shop. In the same breath, we should demand that whatever price we have paid to our suppliers in the past will be lowered more and more in the future, to near zero, until our suppliers simply give us their materials and products. After all, it's a privilege to do business with us.

As consumers, we should demand that all of our products become cheaper and cheaper and cheaper. We should apply the Wal-Mart model to everything in our daily lives and be beneficiaries of this wonderfully eroding price. Whatever we purchase should be less the next time. The price must go down. Why should Wal-Mart get all the profits? Everything should be half price and, the next time we walk into the store, it should be half price of that and, the next time, half price of that—until every price is $0.00. Imagine the ads:

Tiffany 5-carat diamonds:
Today and every day: $0.00. Pick the one you like and give it to your favorite sweetheart today!

The home of your dreams:
8-bedroom, 10,000-square-foot home on your own private 30 acres
Tell us what you want to pay . . . and it's yours!

Just explain the next time you purchase a car, that the price is simply too high. Write a check for half the sticker price and drive away. That is precisely what American businesses do to their suppliers. If a product sells for 90 cents today, it should sell for 10 cents in 3 months. Why shouldn't consumers do exactly the same thing? After all, we are highly important people and businesses should just give us their products.

What should you do, as a business owner, supplier, corporate executive, or consumer, with this information?

- Get your pea shooter and climb the nearest clock tower?
- Set up a hot dog stand and start selling Dodger dogs?
- Make a sex tape and leak it to the media?
- Throw in the towel?
- Try to out-dirty-trick 'em?

Personally, I just can't do any of the above. Despite the challenges of the near-zero-price mentality, manufacturers moving overseas, and a worldwide financial crisis, I try to stay on point and stick to the things I've learned over the years:

BE PREPARED TO WIN.

THINK AHEAD.
STAY CURIOUS.

INVESTIGATE, APPLY, INVENT, BUILD.

LISTEN. ASK QUESTIONS.
FIND OUT IN ADVANCE WHAT THE CUSTOMER
REALLY WANTS.
GIVE THE CUSTOMER MORE VALUE, FREE OF CHARGE.

MAKE THE MOST OF WHATEVER YOU HAVE.
SEE OPPORTUNITY EVERYWHERE.

APPLY THE KNOWLEDGE YOU GAIN.

SWING OUT. TAKE A RISK.
WHAT DO YOU HAVE TO LOSE?

CREATE A COMPANY THAT CAN BUILD TRULY CUSTOM
PRODUCTS, AND SAVE TIME AND MONEY.

UNDO THE COMPLEXITY.
THERE IS POWER IN SIMPLICITY.

BE CLEAR ABOUT YOUR CORE PRINCIPLES
AND STICK TO THEM.

For me and my company, we will continue to build the best products we can with the best materials, sell them at fair prices, be honest, treat people right, and trust that goodwill, ethical business practices, and Yankee ingenuity and determination will prevail.

Afterthoughts:
Television and Two of My Heroes

Afterthoughts:
Television and Two of My Heroes

Television has somewhat of a bad reputation when it comes to parents and their children. How many of our parents encouraged us to watch *more* television? Just about zip, zero, nada.

My parents had interesting reasons for limiting my TV watching. My mom, for instance, did not allow me to watch *Dennis the Menace* because she said Dennis would be a bad influence on me. My dad had other somewhat more sweeping reasons for restricting my TV viewing. He said I could not watch any show that featured "communists." For instance, I was not allowed to watch Art Linkletter because he had decided that Art was a "communist." I think nothing could be further from the truth, but that didn't matter to my dad.

Despite these restrictions, I *was* allowed to watch *some* television—a little after school, one or two shows at night and on Saturday or Sunday afternoon. And, of course, when my parents weren't around, I watched whatever I wanted to watch.

For a kid with such poor reading skills, television opened up a whole new world for me. Certain shows and people I learned about on television I remember to this day because they sparked ideas, made me aware of places I'd never heard of, and stimulated my thinking about how real and imaginary machines and tools could be built.

Two of the people I learned about on TV who stand out in my memories are Jonny Quest and Jim Hall. One was an actual human being; the other, an animated kid who was just as real to me as any kid in the neighborhood.

Jonny Quest

One of the people I most admired when I was growing up was a 10- or 11-year-old kid named Jonny Quest. Jonny wasn't a real person. He was a blond-haired animated TV character who we were supposed to *think* was a real person, and he certainly was real to me.

One of the many cool things about Jonny Quest was that he had his own prime-time, science fiction-adventure TV show named, of course, *Jonny Quest*. The show, produced by Hanna-Barbera, ran from 1964 to 1965 when I was about 6 years old. It was the first animated series to air during prime-time TV and was much more realistic than other Hanna-Barbera cartoon shows such as *The Flintstones* and *The Jetsons*. The show was short lived, apparently due to the high cost of making the highly detailed scenes. At the time, *Jonny Quest* was only marginally successful, but apparently there are legions of fans like me who can't forget it.

Jonny Quest was incredibly cool for several reasons:

A. He had his own TV show.
B. He had an equally cool best friend from India named Hadji.
C. He flew all over the world on adventures with his father, Dr. Benton Quest, a world-renowned scientist.
D. He had a dog, Bandit, who went everywhere with him.
E. To top it all off, he had a bodyguard, a studly guy named Roger "Race" Bannon.

What could be cooler than that?

Jonny, Dr. Quest, Hadji, Bandit, and Race traveled all over the world on adventure after adventure. Everywhere they went, there were bad guys trying to subvert whatever they were doing. They encountered snow creatures, invisible monsters, and gargoyles that came to life. There were scuba divers with knives and underwater spear guns. There were mummies and ghost ships. All of these things are what a boy's memories are made of.

One of the reasons the show had such a big impact on me as a kid was that it made me realize that the world was so much bigger than I thought it was. Up until then, for all I knew the universe consisted of me, my family, my bike, the kids at my school, and the streets around my house at the base of the San Bernardino Mountains. But Jonny and his family traveled all over the world; sometimes, they went to places I'd never heard of before.

They went to the jungle. They were in the desert. They traveled by ship to the Arctic. They went to Egypt. They went to the Himalayas. And Hadji was from India, and I knew very little if anything about India at age 6. Nor had I ever seen or heard of a turban, which Hadji wore all the time.

At the time I didn't fully comprehend why Hadji lived with Jonny and his dad. To me he was just a great friend of Jonny's who was kind of mysterious because of the turban he wore. I eventually learned that Dr. Quest had adopted Hadji from Calcutta, India, so Hadji was Jonny's brother *and* his best friend.

Although Jonny Quest was my favorite character on the show and easy to mimic because he wore a simple dark turtleneck, Hadji was a bit more difficult because he always wore a turban.

One day I made a turban out of a towel and attached a piece of clunky jewelry that was my mom's to the front of the towel to copy the bejeweled piece that Hadji wore. My mom helped me put it on. I wore it outside. I think I even wore it to school once when I was in second or third grade. I thought I was a trendsetter. If Hadji had a turban, it had to be cool.

The *Jonny Quest* show was a geography-science fiction-science lesson all rolled into 30 minutes, once a week for a year. At the end of an episode, I'd get out this big globe that my family had and try to figure out where all of these places were that Jonny had visited.

The other intriguing aspect of the show was the combination of real and imaginary machines, animals, and life situations they encountered. I tried to figure out what was real and what wasn't, and if it something was *not* "real," was it possible?

Science fiction and the paranormal were the theme of many of the episodes, which inspired me to want to know more about the world. It was the first time, for instance, that I'd heard of something called a Yeti when Jonny and his dad were somewhere in the Himalayas and ran into one. They also traveled to the Arctic, which I'd barely heard of at 6 years old, where there was a submarine that could break through the ice, a "snow skimmer," a "snow bus," and other great machines.

One of my favorite episodes had to do with Dr. Erikson, a scientist who had created an anti-gravity device called the Erik-on Bar, a device that was about the length of a man's arm. When plugged into a special machine, the device created an anti-gravity field, so anything above the bar was suspended in mid-air. Bad guys, of course, wanted to steal the device. A gargoyle stole it, but Jonny helped defeat the enemies.

I was particularly struck by the fact that Jonny was interested in science. He also was smart enough to understand what his dad, the scientist, was talking about. The science wasn't beyond him.

The show also made me think about how someone who was young could do adult things. Jonny drove vehicles, he outsmarted the bad guys, he crept into scary places and snuck up on enemies. He showed fear sometimes, but he did what he needed to do anyway. That really stayed with me. Even when you're young, why can't you do things that an adult might do? As improbable as the stories might have been, they inspired me to think outside the norm from things my friends were doing.

Even though Jonny was an animated character, really just a cartoon, what a great role model he was for me as a kid. Jonny Quest was the good guy. He wasn't edgy or sinister. He wasn't an amalgam of a little bit of evil here and there. To the best of my recollection, he never killed or hurt anyone, but he was always clever. He might have had a little-boy mischievous side, but he was the good guy even though he just about always wore a black turtleneck, at least that's what it looked like on my black-and-white television. Bad people attempted to do bad things to him and his father, but he always prevailed. It was a great very early lesson about the value of hard work, smarts, and basic goodness.

Jim Hall

Watching car racing on television was one of my favorite things to do, but even more important than the races themselves was seeing all the crazy new cars created by some of the best innovators in the business. The guy among guys in the world of race-car innovators was Jim Hall.

Being a very poor reader, about the only time I learned anything about Hall or any of the other car designers was through television. For the most part, I was limited to *ABC's Wide World of Sports*, hosted by Jim McKay, which ran for more than 35 years beginning in 1961. The taped program, which featured two or three different sports, always started with those now-famous words about "the thrill of victory" and "the agony of defeat." I would watch the beginning, as everyone did, and the agony of defeat as some poor guy fell off a ski jump.

Wide World of Sports was a great show, but it didn't feature nearly enough car racing as far as I was concerned. The Indianapolis 500, on the other hand, was a couple of hours of TV completely devoted to racing. I watched the show every year from the earliest time I can remember even watching television. It was the highlight of the year in terms of car racing.

Each year I watched with anticipation to see what crazy new vehicle would be at the Indy 500. Rules in the sport changed and things are different today, but for a long time Indy 500 showcased innovations and many, many failed ideas. Unfortunately, some of those innovations cost people their lives; others cost people their careers; and others were just flat slow. But each year I couldn't wait to see what kind of crazy-looking vehicle would show up. Since I had great difficulty with reading, it never occurred to me that there might be a book or magazine on vehicles or racing. I thought that everything there was to know about the subject came through the TV.

I first learned about Jim Hall watching the Indy 500 one year. Hall was the first to come up with the idea of attaching a wing to a race car. A wing creates lift, which of course makes flight possible. However, Hall saw it just the opposite. If the wing was mounted upside down, he reasoned, it would push the car down, which would translate into more traction and faster speeds in the corners. The instant I saw the first wing on a car at Indy, I thought how brilliant Hall was.

Over the years, I recognized that Jim Hall wasn't always at Indy. In fact, had I been able to read at the time, I would have learned that he worked on other race cars and other kinds of racing in addition to the Indy 500.

Hall started a company called Chaparral Cars. One of Hall's most famous Chaparral cars was the Chaparral 2J, affectionately called the *vacuum car*. He mounted a second engine on board, in this case a snowmobile engine, to run a vacuum to suck the car down just prior to the corner. All the driver needed to do as he approached the corner at very high speed was turn on the auxiliary engine and the car would be sucked down, giving it tremendous grip and power as it came around the corner. Like many of Hall's ideas, the vacuum car was highly controversial, in part, I believe, because it was so darn fast, and in short order, it was banned from racing.

Jim Hall also the first to use the principle of *ground effect*—another great term—in car racing. What did it mean? How did he come up with it? How could he be so brilliant? The idea of using wings to push the car down and create grip was a great idea. Using a vacuum to suck the car to the ground was a great idea. Hall combined the two ideas in a ground-effect design, which didn't require a vacuum per se, but instead used the air flowing over and under the car to create a vacuum. Hall's amazing ground effect car had a shape that was absolutely beautiful. The car was painted bright yellow and had a Pennzoil logo midway down the side.

What inspires me to this day about Jim Hall is that he was always innovating, designing, creating, and pushing the envelope, building things that no one else had seen or done before. He didn't sit back and wait for others to invent. He took the lead.

If someone asked the question, "In modern motor racing innovation, who stands out above the rest?" Jim Hall is definitely at the top. It was an American who came up with the ideas. It was an American idea to put wings on cars. It was an American who came up with the greatest innovations in cars. Seeing Hall's incredible cars made me proud to be an American. I was free to think of anything, to come up with anything I could imagine.

Glen Carrio's Glossary

Glen Carrio's Glossary

Cable Divination: A highly sought-after skill requiring a doctorate in paranormal psychology; used to ascertain the details of a cable assembly schematic that is many times removed from the original due to a lack of concern that the potential bidder has any idea what is on the page. After all, it's just a cable.

Cable Swami: A new job that has arisen as a result of declining clarity about product specifications. The skill set includes mind reading, ESP, and the Vulcan Mind Meld.

Cellular Manufacturing: Complete integration of all manufacturing processes to serve a customer.

Cephloid Variable: A go-kart exhaust system with human-like qualities.

China Price: Always half of the U.S. price, and if the U.S. price is half again, then China Price is half of that.

Dyslexia: The ability to see things that no one else sees.

Just-In-Time: Producing only what is needed and delivering it only when it is needed, which is why so many U.S. companies have gone to China. Right.

Lean Manufacturing: Whatever crappy process you use, just add the word "lean" before it, for example, "Lean Really Slow Crappy Service."

Mass Production: For fools who keep themselves busy and have stuff laying around everywhere. Looks highly impressive.

Near-Zero Pricing: When a customer has brought you to this price, you are unceremoniously dropped and the customer starts the same thing over again with someone else.

One Operator =^{TM}: The sum total of my creative genius.

Operator Rate Per Conductor: One-half the sum total of my creative genius.

Over-Molding: At one time, over-molding was the process of using specialty equipment to inject hot plastic over an object to encapsulate, then seal it. Now this means screwing together two or more pieces or gluing one thing to another for easy access or removal later; special equipment no longer required.

Six Sigma: Figures lie, and liars figure.

Statistical Process Control: Meaningless, endless collection of numbers placed on charts to look good to customers, but no actual action is taken.

Total Quality Management (TQM): Any original meaning and value have been overshadowed by more sexy approaches such as "lean."

World Class: No longer exists because low price is all that matters.

GC's Squirrel Outtakes

Confessions of a Dyslexic

Tom Petty look-alike (when I had long hair)

To date:

> Broken bones: 5 ribs, 2 clavicles, 1 tibia, 2 damaged vertebras
> Disease free
> Never smoked a cigarette, no drugs, no meds, no hard liquor ever
> 10½ medium shoe size
> 170 lbs, 7% body fat
> 6 feet, 0" tall
> No college degree
> High school grad to janitor: 1978–1980

Nicknames:

> "Speed"
> "Will"
> "My dog shithead"
> "Ron Dennis"
> "Cable Doctor"
> "The Emperor"
> "Cable god (small g)"
> "The action entrepreneur
>   of the 90s"
> "The Don"
> "Don Carrio"
> "Boss Carrio"

2 speeds: Off and Turbo

Keep in mind: A man can never have enough titanium or carbon fiber.

Lightning Round

Questions and answers from my hypothetical
recent interview with Barbara Walters:

Question:	Answer:
Ginger or Mary Ann?	"Both"
Paper or plastic?	"Nuke the unborn gay whales"
Boxers or briefs?	"Commando"
Best advice given?	"One operator =™"
Best advice taken?	"Jesus Saves"
Best miles per gallon?	" '61 Austin Healey Sprite, 48 mpg"
Ever been a "Sugar Daddy"?	"No, but one day I hope to have my own line of health food bars."
You worked for World Speed Motorsports for no salary. What exactly did you do?	"I was the information czar, spy, and provider of nutritious, delicious snacks."
Spell "entrepreneur"	"Aunt-ra-poo-manure"
Personal championship season?	"1998"
Team championship seasons?	"1998, 1999, 2000, 2001, 2002, 2003, 2006"
Ever been found in a compromised position?	"Yes. Urinating on a competitor's factory in Ireland"
If you could be a tree, what would it be?	"Firewood"
When traveling in coach, what is the square footage allotted?	"Coach? I met Greg T. Nelson once, and introduced my 8-year-old daughter as my wife."

Question:	Answer:
What do ones and zeros mean to you?	"I do not understand the question."
I understand that you are visually and physically challenged. Explain.	"With dyslexia, everything is a challenge, even walking through doors. Right is left; left is right. Besides, with Restless Leg Syndrome, acrophobia, and a fear of any food that's red, what more can I say?"
What is the name of the movie, had it been produced, that would have rocketed you to a teen idol?	"The Perching of Eagles"
When gambling on the ponies, would you go for the Daily Double or the Exacta?	"No question. The Daily Double."
Legend has it that at age 14, you designed a spacecraft to leave Earth to live in a better place. Is that true?	"At the time, I did not know how far away new worlds were. I would have run out of air and food long before I arrived."
Cattle mutilations are up 37.8% in Colorado Springs since Carrio Cabling moved into the area. Is there a link?	"I must go now to feed the alien babies."

Made in the USA
Monee, IL
04 March 2021